Who Says Animals Go To Heaven?

*A Collection Of
Prominent Christian
Leaders' Beliefs
In Life After Death
For Animals*

Niki Behrikis Shanahan

Author Of

*There Is Eternal Life For Animals
Animal Prayer Guide*
and
*The Rainbow Bridge:
Pet Loss Is Heaven's Gain*

Published By:
Pete Publishing
Tyngsborough, Massachusetts

www.eternalanimals.com

Who Says Animals Go To Heaven?

*A Collection Of Prominent
Christian Leaders' Beliefs
In Life After Death
For Animals*

Copyright © 2008 by Niki Behrikis Shanahan

All Rights Reserved. No part of this book may be used or reproduced in any manner without written permission. This book is protected under the copyright laws of the United States of America.

First Published 2008

ISBN-10 Digit: 0972030158
ISBN-13 Digit: 978-0-9720301-5-1

Library of Congress Control Number: 2008925519

Cover design by Sylvia Corbett.

All quotations not in public domain are copyright protected, and used by permission.

Published By:
Pete Publishing
P. O. Box 282
Tyngsborough, MA 01879

www.eternalanimals.com

Table of Contents

Introduction 7
Ministry Commentaries 11
    Arrington, French L. 11
    Baring-Gould, Sabine 13
    Beet, Joseph Agar 15
    Booth, General William 16
    Brown, David 18
    Bruce, Frederick Fyvie 19
    Butler, Joseph 21
    Calvin, John 22
    Carter, Thomas Thellusson 24
    Carter, William 25
    Chalmers, Thomas 26
    Clarke, Adam 27
    Cranfield, C. E. B. 27
    Criswell, W. A. 28
    Darby, John Nelson 30
    De Haan, Martin R. 30
    Ellicott, Charles John 31
    Eyton, Robert 32
    Farrar, Frederic William 33
    Fuller, Andrew 34
    Fulton, John S. 34
    Gurney, John Hampden 35
    Hahne, Harry Alan 36
    Haldane, Robert 37

Hammond, Peter 38
Headlam, Arthur Cayley 41
Henry, Matthew 43
Hitchcock, Edward 44
Hoffman, Frank L. 45
Johnson, Barton W. 45
Josephus, Flavius 46
Keble, John 47
Kirby, H. 49
Lindsay, James Gordon 49
Lloyd-Jones, D. Martyn 50
Luther, Martin 50
MacDonald, George 51
Main, William 53
Marvin, Frederic Rowland 53
McGee, J. Vernon 54
Moor, John Frewen 55
Moorehead, William Gallogly 56
Morris, Francis Orpen 58
Newell, William Reed 59
Pettingill, William Leroy 60
Phillips, Forbes Alexander 61
Pringle, William 62
Pusey, Edward Bouverie 63
Pym, William Wollaston 64
Sanday, William 65
Scott, Thomas 65
Stott, John Robert Walmsley 66
Stifler, James Madison 67

Thomas, William Henry Griffith	68
Toplady, Augustus Montague	69
Trench, Richard Chenevix	70
Van Impe, Jack	71
Walvoord, John F.	71
Wesley, John	72
Williams, Isaac	75
Wood, J. G.	77
Wordsworth, Christopher	83
Zuck, Roy B.	84

Other Commentaries *85*

Carrington, Edith	85
Colam, John	86
Dixon, Royal	86
Springer, Rebecca Ruter	87

Bibliography *90*
Resources *95*

Introduction

> "And He gave some, apostles; and some, prophets; and some, evangelists; and some, pastors and teachers; For the perfecting of the saints, for the work of the ministry, for the edifying of the body of Christ."
>
> Ephesians 4:11-12, KJV

God has appointed apostles, prophets, evangelists, pastors, and teachers to edify the body of Christ, and teach them truths from the Bible. In this book a substantial group of over 60 experts consisting of theologians, scholars, teachers, pastors, evangelists, and missionaries weigh in on the subject of life after death for animals. We can learn a great deal from their spiritual knowledge, education, wisdom, and lifelong commitment and dedication to the study of the Word of God.

When compiled these commentaries make a strong statement about the future life of animals. In view of this substantial collection, and considering that so many people in the ministry today glean over the works of our Christian founding fathers for edification; it's time for our pastors and ministers to take a "fresh look" at this Biblical truth.

These commentaries from Bible experts cross the lines of denominations, and span throughout generations and geographical locations. It reflects only a small percentage of those who believe that animals go to Heaven. It's just a tiny representation, or you might say, "the tip of the iceberg," and is by no means a complete collection of everyone who shares this belief. If I continued to search for additional people to add to this book, it would probably take a lifetime to collect everything I could find, and still it wouldn't be a complete list. Many people have never documented their beliefs, and so it is impossible to determine how widespread the acceptance of this truth is.

The consequences of the fall of humanity involve all of creation. The animals have suffered greatly as a result of man's disobedience to God, and there are great cosmic ramifications. All of creation, including the animals, have hope and wait eagerly because the whole creation will be delivered from corruption.

You can have your own opinion, but you can't have your own facts. John Adams said, "Facts are stubborn things." The facts in the Bible about life after death for animals speak loud and clear. Many may be familiar with one of my earlier books, ***There Is Eternal Life For Animals***, which is a study of the Bible proving that all animals go to Heaven and have eternal life. Now I submit these opinions as further support and confirmation on the subject. As you will see, they have some very interesting light to shed on this truth. I have arranged these commentaries in alphabetical order, and I've included a brief biography of each individual. Many of the comments that you will read are based on Romans 8:18-23, therefore, I would like to give you those Scriptures to make it convenient for you to reference them. First, I'll start with the King James Version since most people reference that version. Then I'll follow-up with The Living Bible Version from 1971 for a clearer understanding, which interestingly uses the word "animals."

> "18. For I reckon that the sufferings of this present time are not worthy to be compared with the glory which shall be revealed in us.
>
> 19. For the earnest expectation of the creature waiteth for the manifestation of the sons of God.
>
> 20. For the creature was made subject to vanity, not willingly, but by reason of him who hath subjected the same in hope,

21. Because the creature itself also shall be delivered from the bondage of corruption into the glorious liberty of the children of God.

22. For we know that the whole creation groaneth and travaileth in pain together until now.

23. And not only they, but ourselves also, which have the firstfruits of the Spirit, even we ourselves groan within ourselves, waiting for the adoption, to wit, the redemption of our body."

Romans 8:18-23, King James Version.

"18-19. Yet what we suffer now is nothing compared to the glory He will give us later. For all creation is waiting patiently and hopefully for that future day when God will resurrect His children.

20-21. For on that day thorns and thistles, sin, death, and decay – the things that overcame the world against its will at God's command – will all disappear, and the world around us will share in the glorious freedom from sin which God's children enjoy.

22. For we know that even the things of nature, like animals and plants, suffer in sickness and death as they await this great event.

23. And even we Christians, although we have the Holy Spirit within us as a foretaste of future glory, also groan to be released from pain and suffering. We, too, wait anxiously for that day when God will give us our full rights as His children, including the new bodies He has promised us – bodies that will never be sick again and will never die."

Romans 8:18-23, The Living Bible

We have some very distinguished writers who have penned famous hymns, such as, Augustus Toplady, who wrote *Rock of Ages*, General William Booth's *Send The Fire*, Martin Luther's

A Mighty Fortress Is Our God, William Newell who wrote *At Calvary*, and *Onward Christian Soldiers* by Sabine Baring-Gould. A very popular devotional booklet today called *Our Daily Bread* is published by RBC Ministries, which was founded by one of our writers, Martin R. De Haan.

While most of these people have already gone home to be with the Lord, we have some present day writers, such as, French Arrington, who is currently Professor Emeritus of New Testament Greek and Exegesis at the Church of God Theological Seminary. I had the pleasure of talking to French Arrington on the telephone, and we were discussing the fact that some people seemed to think that eternal life for animals was a new belief, but in fact it goes back throughout the centuries.

Peter Hammond is a missionary, author, and the Founder and Director of Frontline Fellowship. Jack Van Impe is an evangelist who appears on his weekly television show *Jack Van Impe Presents* with his wife, Rexella. Frank Hoffman is a retired Jewish-United Methodist Pastor, who with his wife, Mary, are the founders of The Mary T. and Frank L. Hoffman Family Foundation. And, Harry Hayne is Associate Professor of New Testament Studies at Golden Gate Baptist Theological Seminary, Scottsdale, Arizona.

One of my favorite commentaries is from W. A. Criswell who says, "The whole creation of God will be delivered from corruption, and that includes our pets. That includes our animals." Three of the entries from William Carter, John Fulton, and Forbes Alexander Phillips, appeared in newspaper articles.

As you will see, the immortality of animals is definitely not a new belief. This truth has been a known fact since the Bible was written. This is a very exciting and revealing collection of commentaries, so now please join me in this amazing spiritual journey.

Ministry Commentaries

Arrington, French L.

1931 – Tennessee. French L. Arrington, Ph.D., is noted in the Evangelical and Pentecostal movement as a theologian, teacher, and author. He attended Lee College, Cleveland, TN 1953-1955. B.A., University of Chattanooga, Chattanooga, TN. Major: Psychology, Minor: Languages 1957. Master of Divinity Columbia Theological Seminary, Decatur, GA 1960. ThM. Columbia Theological Seminary, Decatur, GA. Thesis: *The Evidence of Immortality in This Present Mortal Condition as Reflected in II Corinthians 4:18-5:10*, 1968. Ph.D. St. Louis University, St. Louis, MO. Biblical Languages with specialization in the Pauline Corpus. Dissertation: *Paul's Aeon Theology in I Corinthians*, 1975. He has served as a Pastor and for seventeen years was on the faculty of Lee University, where he was Chairman of the Department of Bible and Theology and received the Excellence in Teaching Award.

Dr. Arrington is well known for his published works on the New Testament. He was on the editorial committee for *Life in the Spirit Study Bible,* and was a general editor of the *Life in the Spirit New Testament Commentary,* and contributor of the exposition on Luke-Acts in the commentary — all published by Zondervan.

Dr. Arrington has taught at Lee University and the Church of God Theological Seminary, both in Cleveland, Tennessee. Currently he is Professor Emeritus of New Testament Greek and Exegesis at the Church of God Theological Seminary.

> "Creation's fate is intimately tied to man's fate. The redemption of the rational creature will accomplish also the redemption of all of creation. Thus creation shares with man in the hope of ultimate salvation." (Page 17)

"It is clear from our review of Romans 8:19-22 that redemption for Paul is a concept of cosmic redemption, just as the doctrine of the Fall. In this pericope Paul does not relate the Fall; but he assumes that when man, the head of creation, fell the world fell with him. This theme of the solidarity of man and creation, which is prominent in apocalyptic and Old Testament prophecy, indicates that the natural world, as well as man, stands in need of redemption."

"Paul makes no allowance for the annihilation of the present material universe on the day of redemption. Rather than the replacement of the natural world by a completely new world, Paul envisions the transformation of the animate and inanimate creation so that it will be returned to the service of God's glory."

"Since man and the whole creation are bound together in redemption as well as in sin, all creation eagerly awaits the unveiling of the sons of God, because it has been subjected to 'sin-vanity' and consequently is frustrated in the fulfillment of the purpose for which God created it. This, of course, is not any fault of its own but is due to man's alienation from God. God, however, has left creation hope that it will be freed from subservience to change and decay and introduced into the freedom which is the state of the glory of the children of God. Creation now utters concerted groans under the burden of the consequences of man's sin, but this groaning is a sign of expectation, of entering into the redemptive benefits of the children of God and sharing in their teleology."

"Hence, in short, the emphasis of Romans 8:19-22 is quite clear – the eschatological redemption of the natural world." (Pages 27-28)

Arrington, French L., *Creation's Hopeful Expectation: An Exegesis of Romans 8:19-22*, 1972, Tennessee.

Baring-Gould, Sabine

1834 – 1924, England. An author and scholar, he was educated at Clare College, Cambridge, and made Master of Arts in 1860. He was Curate of Horbury, Yorkshire in 1864, Vicar of Dalton in 1866, and Rector of East Mersea, Essex in 1871. He is remembered particularly as a writer of hymns, the best-known being *Onward Christian Soldiers.*

"The great truth held up to us this day is the Creation of the world by God. *By Whom* the world was made – that is a truth which we all hold. But there is another truth involved in it, spoken of in the text, to which we do not give equal attention. *For Whom* was the world made? – For Him of Whom St. Paul is here speaking, for Jesus Christ. The world was made, not for Adam and Eve, but for Jesus Christ. For Him the sun was kindled and casts his heat and light through the universe. For Jesus Christ the moon circles round the earth, and sheds her white beams at night. For Jesus Christ the stars twinkle, and the planets burn with steady light. For Jesus Christ the buds open in spring, and the birds twitter in the bushes. Look about as you go through the churchyard on your way home, and mark the early daisies. Those white rays tipped with crimson, spread about that little golden heart for Jesus Christ. What a mystery is this! What does it mean? Can it be true? – There is no doubt about that – 'All things were created *by* Him, and *for* Him.'"

"If we take another passage of St. Paul's writings we may get to understand this mystery better. St. Paul in the Epistle to the Romans (Chapter 8) says, 'I reckon that the sufferings of this present time are not worthy to be compared with the glory which shall be revealed in us.' This observation leads him to a new subject, to a consideration of the circumstances of this glory. 'For,' he continues 'the earnest expectation of the creature waiteth for the manifestation of the sons of God.' That is, Creation is in a state of expectancy, and the object of this expectancy is the revelation of the sons of God, in the glory of their resurrection bodies. The Apostle then goes on to explain the cause of this earnest expectation of all Creation. He says, 'The creature was made subject to vanity, – not willingly, – but by reason of Him who hath subjected the same in hope.' By which this is meant: – all created beings became subject to death and corruption, not of their own accord, nor through their own sin, but through the wilful sin of Adam. They fell with Adam, and were suffered so to fall, that all creatures might be united with man in one hope, that hope being man's restoration. Man is the key stone of nature's arch, the final link of the chain of the six days, uniting that work to God. By the fall of man the whole substructure of Creation was injured, the arch of nature crumbled down, the chain of created beings fell to the ground."

"But God purposes man's restoration, and the Apostle shows us that man's restoration will be the restoration of all nature. He says 'He hath subjected the same in hope,' and then adds the remarkable words, 'Because the creature also shall be delivered from the bondage of corruption, into the glorious liberty of the Children of God.' By man came death, and death brings corruption. The shadow of man's sin has darkened the bright face of nature, the burden of his sin is on all creation, and it groans. 'We know that the whole creation groaneth and travaileth in pain together until now' – in other words, corruption has eaten deep into all created nature and saddened its old brightness."

"Truly, the whole creation does groan and travail in pain together, – but not forever; with man's restoration comes the regeneration of all creation."

Fowle, Edmund, **Plain Preaching For A Year**, 1873, *The Future Of Creation* by Rev. S. Baring-Gould, M.A., W. Skeffington, Piccadilly, London.

Beet, Joseph Agar

1840 – 1924, England. Joseph Agar Beet was an English Wesleyan. He was a Pastor from 1864 to 1885, and Professor of Systematic Theology in Wesleyan College, Richmond, 1885-1905. He was also a member of the Faculty of Theology in the University of London in 1901-05. Beet published widely in the field of Biblical studies, particularly the writings of St. Paul, on which he published many commentaries.

"Nature is prevented from putting forth its powers, from manifesting its real grandeur, and from attaining its original destiny. It is therefore bound. And its bondage is caused by the necessary decay of its products. All that Nature brings forth is doomed to die. And Nature is compelled to slay its own offspring. The lightning flash destroys the stately oak. The winter's cold kills the songsters of the summer. Animals devour other animals to maintain life. And this universal destruction limits the achievements of Nature. Instead of constant growth, Nature's beauty and strength fade away. The powers of the material Creation are bound by fetters of decay."

"The freedom of etc., with which the *children of God* will be made free in the day when their glory (verse 17) will be revealed. This freedom, Creation will share. The bondage of corruption was designed to last only for a time. It was imposed when man fell; and will be removed when man's redemption is complete (verse

23). Paul carries on his personification by saying that, when Nature was made to share *the bondage* which resulted from man's sin, a *hope* was given to it of sharing the liberty which will follow man's deliverance."

    Beet, Joseph Agar, ***A Commentary On St. Paul's Epistle To The Romans***, Third Revised Edition, 1882, Hodder and Stoughton, London.

Booth, General William

1829 – 1912, England. We're all familiar with the Christian organization, The Salvation Army, and the wonderful work that it does. For almost 100 years The Salvation Army's trained employees and volunteers have served at disasters, which place a community at risk or destroy family security and well-being. Counseling survivors, consoling the injured and distressed, comforting the bereaved, conducting funeral and memorial services, chaplaincy services to staff and volunteers. Where needed, mobile feeding units serve hot meals to survivors and relief personnel. Shelters may be established and maintained in Salvation Army facilities or other sites. Programs include childcare, to allow adult family members to salvage personal effects, apply for long-term assistance, schedule reconstruction, and undertake other necessary tasks.

General William Booth was the Founder and 1st General of The Salvation Army, one of the most respected organizations in the world. Booth was a preacher at Binfield Chapel in Clapham, England, for the Reformers (Wesleyan Reform Union). He was a Methodist Minister, author, and he wrote the hymn **"Send The Fire."** William Booth entitled a volume of some of his prophetic encounters ***"Visions."***

General Booth had several visions of Heaven. In his rare antiquarian and out-of-print book called ***Visions*** dated 1906, General Booth records the following vision that he had:

"I have had another vision. I thought I was safe landed in Heaven, where I had settled down all at once, quite at my ease, everything appearing so familiar and home-like. It was a lovely place, strongly resembling in many respects the fairest of the countries I have traveled over during my salvation campaigns down here, and yet as far beyond them in every form of beauty and every source of delight as can possibly be conceived."

"The blue skies, the towering mountains, the green valleys, the shady groves, the luxuriant vineyards, the charming flowers, the flowing rivers – I did not observe any sea – were all exquisitely beautiful beyond the power of language to describe. Then in, about, and indeed everywhere, were the loveliest of birds and the most graceful of animals, and I know not what else."

"I was enraptured with the scene. I was certainly a little surprised to find these living creatures here, having been always rather skeptical as to the resurrection of the animal world. There, however, they certainly were."

Booth, William, *Visions*, 1906, The Salvation Army Printing Works, St. Albans, pages 42-43.

On the Salvation Army website they have an article entitled *"The Life of General William Booth."* In this article we learn that he enjoyed his sons' enthusiasm for animals. It states that, "If a man of one idea, and that idea a burning consciousness of the existence of a God, can be said to have a hobby, the hobby of William Booth was this boyish delight in the pets of a back-garden."

The General's wife, Catherine Booth, grew up loving animals, especially dogs and horses, and could not bear to see any one ill-treat them. General Booth's daughter, Evangeline, became 'The Commander' in the U.S. Evangeline was loudly outspoken against cruelty to animals.

Brown, David

1803 – 1897, Scotland. He studied at the University of Aberdeen (M.A., 1821); was licensed in 1826, and was assistant to Edward Irving in London 1830–32; was ordained Minister of a country chapel six miles southwest of Banff in 1836. He went with the Free Church in 1843, and the same year became Minister of St. James', Glasgow; was elected professor of apologetics, church history, and exegesis of the Gospels at the Free Church College, Aberdeen, 1857; elected principal in 1876. He was a director of the National Bible Society of Scotland, one of the founders of the Evangelical Alliance, was deeply interested in the Alliance of the Reformed Churches, and a member of the third General Council at Belfast, 1888. He was moderator of the General Assembly of the Free Church in 1885. Besides numerous contributions to the periodicals, he published *Christ's Second Coming: Will it be Premillenial?* (Edinburgh, 1846; 6th ed., 1867). He collaborated with R. Jamieson and A. R. Fausset in preparing the *Commentary, Critical, Experimental, and Practical, on the Old and New Testaments* (6 vols., Glasgow, 1864–70), furnishing the portion devoted to the Gospels, the Acts, and the Epistle to the Romans; wrote the commentary on the Epistles to the Corinthians for Schaff's Popular Commentary on the New Testament in 1882; and prepared the Epistle to the Romans for Dods and Whyte's Handbooks for Bible Classes Edinburgh, 1883.

> "For the creature — 'the creation' was made subject to vanity, not willingly — that is, through no natural principle of decay. The apostle, personifying creation, represents it as only submitting to the vanity with which it was smitten, on man's account, in obedience to that superior power which had mysteriously linked its destinies with man's. And so he adds but by reason of him who hath subjected *the same* —'who subjected it' in hope — or 'in hope that' because the creature itself also —'even the creation itself' shall be delivered from

the bondage of corruption — its bondage to the principle of decay, into the glorious liberty — rather, 'the liberty of the glory' of the children of God. That is, the creation itself shall, in a glorious sense, be delivered into that freedom from debility and decay in which the children of God, when raised up in glory, shall expatiate: into this freedom from corruptibility the creation itself shall, in a glorious sense, be delivered."

"For we know that the whole creation groaneth and travaileth in pain together until now. If for man's sake alone the earth was cursed, it cannot surprise us that it should share in his recovery. And if so, to represent it as sympathizing with man's miseries, and as looking forward to his complete redemption as the period of its own emancipation from its present sin-blighted condition, is a beautiful thought, and in harmony with the general teaching of Scripture on the subject. And not only they, but ourselves also — or 'not only [so], but even we ourselves'— that is, besides the inanimate creation, waiting for the manifestation of our adoption, to wit, the redemption of our body from the grave: 'not (be it observed) the deliverance of ourselves from the body, but the redemption of the body itself from the grave.'"

Brown, David; Jamieson, Robert; Fausset, A. R., ***Commentary, Critical, Experimental, and Practical, on the Old and New Testaments,*** *The Epistle of Paul the Apostle to the Romans,* 1871. Christian Classics Ethereal Library, Calvin College, Michigan, www.ccel.org.

Bruce, Frederick Fyvie

1910 – 1990, England. (F. F. Bruce) F. F. Bruce, M.A., D.D., was a Bible Scholar, and one of the founders of the modern evangelical understanding of the Bible. His work *New Testament Documents: Are They Reliable?* is considered a classic in the discipline of Christian apologetics. He was born in Elgin, Moray, and was educated at the University of Aberdeen, Cambridge University, and the University of Vienna. After teaching Greek for several years first at the University of Edinburgh and then at the University of Leeds he became head of the Department of Biblical History and Literature at the University of Sheffield in 1947. In 1959 he moved to the University of Manchester where he became professor of Biblical Criticism and Exegesis. In his career he wrote some thirty-three books, and served as editor of *The Evangelical Quarterly* and the *Palestine Exploration Quarterly*. He retired from teaching in 1978.

Bruce was a distinguished Scholar on the life and ministry of the Apostle Paul, and wrote several studies, the best known of which is *Paul: Apostle of the Heart Set Free.* He also wrote commentaries on several Biblical books including *Acts of the Apostles, 1 & 2 Corinthians, the Epistle to the Hebrews,* and *The Epistle Of Paul To The Romans.*

He was honoured with two scholarly works by his colleagues and former students, one to mark his sixtieth and the other to mark his seventieth birthday. He was elected a Fellow of the British Academy, and served as President of the Society for Old Testament Study, and also as President of the Society for New Testament Study. He is one of a handful of Scholars thus recognized by his peers in both fields.

> "But it is not only Christians who have this hope of glory. All creation, says Paul, is waiting with earnest longing for the day when the sons of God will be manifested in glory. Like man, creation must be redeemed because, like man, creation has been subject to a fall."
>
> "This doctrine of the cosmic fall is implicit in the Biblical record from Genesis 3 (where the ground is cursed for man's sake) to Revelation 22 (where 'there shall be no more curse'); and is demanded by any

world-outlook which endeavors to do justice to the Biblical doctrine of creation and the facts of life as we know them. Man is part of nature, and the whole 'nature' of which he forms part was created good, has been subjected to frustration and futility by sin, and will ultimately be redeemed. It is no accident that the redemption of nature is here seen as coinciding with the redemption of man's body – that physical part of his being which links him with the material creation. Man was put in charge of the 'lower' creation and involved it with him when he fell; through the redemptive work of the 'second man' the entail of the fall is broken not only for man himself but for the creation which is dependent on him."

"When Isaiah looked forward to the peaceful coexistence of wolf and lamb in the messianic age, he voiced his hope in the language of poetry, but his poetry enshrines no pathetic fallacy but something much more Biblical and substantial: 'They shall not hurt or destroy in all My holy mountain; for the earth shall be full of the knowledge of the Lord as the waters cover the sea (Is. 11:9, RSV).'"

>Bruce, F. F., *The Epistle Of Paul To The Romans*, 1980, Wm. B. Eerdmans Publishing Company, Michigan, pages 168-169.

Butler, Joseph

1692 – 1752, England. Bishop Butler was an English Bishop, Theologian, Apologist, and Philospher. He was born in England. He entered the Church of England, and went to Oxford. After holding various other preferments he became Rector of the rich living of Stanhope. He was appointed Bishop of Bristol in 1738, and in 1750 he became Bishop of Durham.

"Perhaps after all, the strongest argument from Holy Scripture in favor of the immortality of the brute creation may be found in the Epistle of St. Paul to the Romans, in which (Romans 8:19) he speaks of the 'earnest expectation of the creature' (not man only) waiting 'for the manifestation of the sons of God.' 'The creature itself,' he says, 'was made subject to vanity' ... but shall be delivered from the bondage of corruption into the glorious liberty of the children of God. For we know that 'the whole creation groaneth and travaileth in pain together until now,' waiting until the Lord 'shall save both man and beast.' (Psalm 36:6) We may indeed well believe that as the Gospel has to be preached to every creature, and as the preaching of the Gospel teaches men to be more kind to the lower animals, elevating their present condition, so likewise in that state in which the Kingdom of Christ will be fully perfected and established, the whole animal world will have share in that everlasting and unspeakable blessedness."

>Moor, J. Frewen, ***Thoughts Regarding The Future State Of Animals***, from *Analogy of Religion*, 1899, Warren & Son Printers and Publishers, London, pages 42-44.

Calvin, John

1509 – 1564, France. A French Protestant Theologian during the Protestant Reformation who was a central developer of the system of Christian theology called Calvinism. Calvin was born in France, studied Latin at Paris, and attained a Doctor of Law degree at Orleans, where he developed his interest in theology. Calvin served as a Pastor in Strasbourg, France. He founded the Academy of Geneva in 1559, which was a model for other academies around the world, and eventually became the University of Geneva. He produced many volumes of commentary on most of the books of the Bible. These commentaries have proved to be of lasting value to students of the Bible, and they are still in print after over 400 years.

An excerpt from John Calvin's Commentary on Romans:

> "I understand the passage to have this meaning – that there is no element and no part of the world which, being touched, as it were, with a sense of its present misery, does not intensely hope for a resurrection. He indeed lays down two things, – that all are creatures in distress, – and yet that they are sustained by hope. And it hence also appears how immense is the value of eternal glory, that it can excite and draw all things to desire it."

> "Further, the expression, *expectation expects,* or waits for, though somewhat unusual, yet has a most suitable meaning; for he meant to intimate, that all creatures, seized with great anxiety and held in suspense with great desire, look for that day which shall openly exhibit the glory of the children of God."

> "For to vanity has the creation, etc. He shows the object of expectation from what is of an opposite character; for as creatures, being now subject to corruption, cannot be restored until the sons of God shall be wholly restored; hence they, longing for their renewal, look forward to the manifestation of the celestial kingdom."

> "God has given to everything its charge; and He has not only by a distinct order commanded what He would to be done, but also implanted inwardly the hope of renovation. He has given them a hope of a better condition; with this they sustain themselves, deferring their desire, until the incorruption promised to them shall be revealed."

> "It hence also appears to what excelling glory the sons of God shall be exalted; for all creatures shall be

> renewed in order to amplify it, and to render it illustrious."

> "For creatures are subject to corruption, not through their natural desire, but through the appointment of God, and then, as they have a hope of being hereafter freed from corruption, it hence follows, that they groan like a woman in travail until they shall be delivered. The meaning is, that creatures are not content in their present state, and yet that they are not so distressed that they pine away without a prospect of a remedy, but that they are as it were in travail; for a restoration to a better state awaits them."
>
>> Calvin, John, ***Commentary on Romans***,
>> Christian Classics Ethereal Library, Calvin
>> College, Michigan, www.ccel.org.

Carter, Thomas Thellusson

1808 – 1901, England. (Often known as T. T. Carter or T.T.C.) Carter was a significant figure in the Victorian Church of England, responsible for introducing some Anglo-Catholic practices into the Church. He also founded several charitable organizations. He was a prolific writer on church matters, and a project exists to collect and collate all his writings. For 36 years he was a Rector of Clewer, and an Honorary Curate of Christ Church, Oxford.

> "We may, moreover, connect with the Resurrection of our Lord, the hoped for restoration of the entire creation. For the whole world looks forward to a future state, as the Scripture says: – 'The whole creation groaneth and travaileth in pain together,' and then adds: the 'hope' that 'the creature itself also shall be delivered from the bondage of corruption into the glorious liberty of the children of God.' As the whole world of creation around us suffers from the effects of the fall, so, in some mystery, they will know a

resurrection, and be transformed into a pure, more blessed, more beautiful state. All around will share in some measure in the consequences of the Resurrection of Jesus Christ: we are 'the first fruits' and shall become the 'image of His Person.' But certainly Holy Scripture shows that the living things around us – even animal creatures are not to be destroyed, but after their manner, according to their kind, to be restored, giving praise and glory to 'Him Who created them.'"

> Moor, J. Frewen, ***Thoughts Regarding The Future State Of Animals***, An extract from *Parish Teachings* by Rev. Canon T. T. Carter, 1899, Warren & Son Printers and Publishers, London, pages 77-78.

Carter, William

1868 – unknown. New York. Dr. William Carter was born in England. He was an author, lecturer, and the Pastor of Throop Avenue Presbyterian Church on Macon Street in Brooklyn, New York from 1915 to 1933. Attended Parsons College in Iowa, and McCormick Theological Seminary in Chicago. He received his M.A. in 1894, Ph.D. in 1900, and D.D. in 1906.

An excerpt from a *New York Times* article dated January 31, 1927 in reference to a recent sermon given by Dr. William Carter. The headline read: ***Expects To Meet Animals In Heaven.*** Here is an excerpt from that article.

"Life, not being created but given – as part of an eternal being – animals are as eternal as man. Being eternal, Heaven is as unthinkable without animals as without flowers, or without God. Death is not a goal but a gateway to another and more glorious part of our lives. Immortality is not an end nor a beginning; it is a continuance of life under right circumstances."

> Carter, William, ***Expects To Meet Animals In Heaven***, January 31, 1927, *New York Times*.

Chalmers, Thomas

1780 – 1847, Scotland. Thomas Chalmers was a Scottish mathematician, a leader of the Free Church of Scotland, and author. At the age of eleven Chalmers was entered as a student at St. Andrews, where he devoted himself almost exclusively to mathematics. In January 1799 he was licensed as a Preacher of the Gospel by the St. Andrews presbytery. In May 1803, after attending further courses of lectures in Edinburgh, and acting as assistant to the professor of mathematics at St. Andrews, he was ordained as Minister of Kilmany, about 9 miles from the university town, where he continued to lecture. He was highly regarded during his lifetime as a Natural Theologian. In 1815 he became Minister of the Tron Church, Glasgow, and in 1819 he became Minister of the church and parish of St. John. In 1823, after eight years of work at high pressure, he was glad to accept the chair of moral philosophy at St. Andrews University. In November 1828 he was transferred to the chair of theology in Edinburgh. In 1843, 470 clergymen withdrew from the general assembly, and constituted themselves the Free Church of Scotland, with Dr. Chalmers as moderator.

> "The creation is now waiting, as if in the attitude of earnest expectancy, for that era – when, transformed into a new Heavens and a new earth, it shall become a suitable habitation for those who are declared and manifested to be the sons of God. For creation, then to be so gloriously restored, has for a time been made subject to vanity not willingly on the part at least of any who now live but by reason of him who by his fata disobedience hath brought it into this bondage – yet it is a bondage that is mingled and alleviated with hope; and that too a warranted hope, because creation shall also be delivered from the bondage of corruption: And emancipated from those fetters which now bind and burden and make it impracticable and ungracious, it will come forth in smiles that shall be perennial and

immortal, it will yield a grateful compliance to the wishes of its happy inmates, and have in all its operations the beneficent flow and freedom of God's own children."

Chalmers, Thomas, *Lectures Of The Epistle Of Paul The Apostle To The Romans*, 1874, Robert Carter & Brothers, New York.

Clarke, Adam

1760 or 1762 – 1832, England. British Methodist Theologian and Biblical Scholar. He is chiefly remembered for writing a commentary on the Bible which took him forty years to compile, and which was a primary Methodist theological resource for two centuries.

Adam Clarke's Commentary on Psalm 104:30.

"Thou sendest forth Thy Spirit, they are created, 'They are created again.' And Thou renewest the face of the earth. Do not these words plainly imply a resurrection of the bodies which have died, been dissolved, or turned to dust? And is not the brute creation principally intended here? Is it not on this account it is said, verse 31, 'the glory of the Lord shall endure for ever, (μlw[l leolam,)' to be manifest in those times which are secret, when Jehovah Himself shall rejoice in His works; when the brute creation shall be delivered from the bondage of its corruption? See the notes on Romans 8:19-23."

Clarke, Adam, *The Holy Bible, Containing The Old And New Testaments With A Commentary And Critical Notes by Adam Clarke, LL.D., F.A.S.*, 1854, William Tegg And Co, London.

Cranfield, C. E. B.

1915 – England. (Charles Ernest Burland Cranfield, MA, DD, FBA, Theology) Professor Cranfield is one of the best-known

New Testament Scholars in the world. Professor emeritus of theology at the University of Durham in England, he served as an Army Chaplain in World War II, as a Pastor to prisoners of war, and as a Minister before teaching theology for thirty years (1950-1980).

> "The implication of these verses (Romans 18-23) is surely that Paul sees the coming glory of believers not by itself but accompanied by the glorious liberation of the whole sub-human creation – with a noble breadth and generosity of vision and sympathy such as may be expected of one who truly, and therefore sincerely and intelligently, believes in God as Creator. The liberation which Paul foresees for the creation at the time of the revelation of the sons of God is liberation 'from the bondage of decay,' that is, from the condition of being the slaves of death and decay, of corruption and transitoriness, which is the very opposite of the condition of glory."
>
> "When at last the children of God are made manifest, the sub-human creation will receive again its proper liberty, the liberty of each several part of it, whether animate or inanimate, fully and perfectly to fulfill its Creator's purpose for it – the liberty which is denied to it so long as man is unready to play his part in the great drama of God's praise."
>
> Cranfield, C. E. B., ***Romans A Shorter Commentary***, 1985, William B. Eerdmans Publishing Company, Michigan, pages 197-198.

Criswell, W. A.

1909 – 2002, Oklahoma. (Wallie Amos Criswell, Ph.D.). Dr. W. A. Criswell was twice elected President of the Southern Baptist Convention (SBC), from 1968 to 1969. Dr. Criswell published fifty-four books, including an annotated Criswell Study Bible. He received eight honorary doctorates. He founded Criswell College, First Baptist Academy, and KCBI Radio. He served on the board of trustees of Baylor University, Baylor Health Care System, Dallas Baptist University, and The Baptist Standard. He also served as a member of the Annuity Board and as Chairman of the Trustees of the Baptist Sunday School Board (now LifeWay Christian Resources). The Baptist Banner characterized his contribution to the Southern Baptist Convention as 'historic.'

At age 10 he professed faith in Christ at a revival meeting. By the time he was 12 he made a public commitment of his life to the gospel ministry, delivering his first sermon as the funeral message for a beloved pet dog.

> "Now, Romans 8:19-23 avows the deliverance of the whole creation – all of it. The burnt-out planets and these barren desserts, fallen humanity and all of creation will be delivered. The word *ktisis*, 'creation,' is used as the subject in verses 19, 20, 21 and 23. The whole creation of God will be delivered from corruption, and that includes our pets. That includes our animals. It's the whole work of our creative God. There's going to be a beautiful Edenic Paradise for us all – for us and for them."
>
> Criswell, W. A., *"What I Believe About Heaven: The Inexpressible Preciousness,"* June 24, 1990, www.wacriswell.org, Texas.

"The title of the message is: 'Redemptive suffering.' In the re-creation of the world – for the world shall be re-created, all of it: the firmament above, and the earth below, the fowls that fly, the fish that swim, the little creatures that creep, and the man who walks in the earth, the flower that buds, the tree that dies, the grass of the fields – everything that God has made will be remade. All that God has created will be re-created. There shall be a new Heaven and a new earth."

"... There is to be a new day. There is to be a new day for all of this world; not just for the humanity, not just for the people. But for all of God's creation. All of God's world is to be delivered out of the bondage of corruption."

>Criswell, W. A., ***Redemptive Suffering***, 10/17/54, www.wacriswell.org, Texas.

Darby, John Nelson

1800 – 1882, England, Ireland. Darby was an Anglo-Irish Evangelist, Bible Commentator, and Clergyman who was born in London. He studied at Westminster School and Trinity College, Dublin. For a couple of years he was an Anglican Clergyman. In 1825, Darby was ordained Deacon of the established Church of Ireland, and the following year as Priest. In 1830 he was the principal Founder of the Plymouth Brethren. He used his classical skills to translate the Bible from the original texts. In English he wrote a Synopsis of the Bible, and many other scholarly religious articles. He wrote hymns and poems.

In John Nelson Darby's commentary on Romans he says when the glory shall set the children free that even the creature shall be delivered from the bondage of corruption, and partake and share in the liberty of the glory. He says it was not the will of the creature which made it subject, but on account of him who subjected it, on account of man.

De Haan, Martin R.

1891 – 1965, Michigan. Dr. Martin R. De Haan was a well-respected Bible teacher and commentator, pastor, author, and physician. He was the founder of Radio Bible Class (RBG Ministries). De Haan graduated from Hope College in Michigan, and the University of Illinois College of Medicine.

RBC Ministries publishes *Our Daily Bread*, one of the most widely read devotional booklets printed today, with over 10 million per issue, in 37 languages. They also publish *My Utmost for His Highest, The Discovery Series.* RBC radio produces the radio programs; *Discover The Word, Words to Live By;* and *Walk in the Word* with Dr. James MacDonald. Another ministry produced by RBC is a television program, Day of Discovery, hosted by Mart De Haan and Jimmy DeYoung.

> "The Bible tells us that this creation also must be delivered from the curse of sin. Many passages present this much-neglected truth, but Romans 8 alone should be enough to establish this fact. When Christ died on Calvary He died not only to save us from going to hell, but He saved us to reign with Him on the earth. He did even more, however, He died not only for sinners but He died to redeem the entire creation. It, too, must be redeemed from the curse. The animal creation shall also share in the deliverance of the Redeemer who opens the seven-sealed book."
>
> De Haan, M. R., ***Studies in Revelation***, 1946, Published by Kregel Publications, Grand Rapids, Michigan, pages 112-114. Used by permission of the publisher. All rights reserved.

Ellicott, Charles John

1819 – 1905, England. Bishop Ellicott was a British Clergyman and Scholar. He was Professor of Divinity at King's College, London (1858), Cambridge (1860), Bishop of Gloucester and Bristol, and chairman for 11 years of the New Testament Revision Committee.

> ***"The Destiny of the Creature:*** It is desirable to retain steadily in view the intimate connection between man and the animal and material world. In the very first day of his creation, man is indissolubly associated with nature. Not only is he to have dominion over all that liveth, but he is to subdue and make his own the earth

he treads on. When he falls, the earth becomes cursed; when the deluge sweeps off his race, the guiltless animals perish with him; when the covenant is made with the solitary surviving family, the surviving creatures are specially included in its provisions: the fowl and the cattle, and every living creature of all flesh, share the blessings of the Divine clemency. Even so it is impossible to doubt that when the restitution of man takes place, the restitution of the earth and its occupants will speedily and immediately follow."

>Moor, J. Frewen, ***Thoughts Regarding The Future State Of Animals***, from University sermons on ***The Destiny of the Creature***, 1899, Warren & Son Printers and Publishers, London, page 87.

Eyton, Robert

1845 – 1908, England. Rev. Robert Eyton, M.A., graduated at Christ Church, Oxford, in 1869, ordained in 1870. He became Rector of Holy Trinity at Upper Chelsea in 1884.

"We think of animals as being objects of God's creative love, and at once it puts us in a new relation towards them. It gives us a new hope about their future; it gives us a glimpse of that tremendous hope which seems to have taken hold of the mind of St. Paul, and to have helped him to see how the 'earnest expectation of the creature waiteth for the manifestation of the sons of God.' – how all those great and wonderful scenes which display the vastness of natural forces look forward in their grandeur and beauty to the time when man shall not only be, but be declared to be, the Son of that Father who is at once the 'All Sovereign,' and the 'Maker of Heaven and Earth.'"

>Moor, J. Frewen, ***Thoughts Regarding The Future State Of Animals***, extract from a

sermon entitled "*Our Brute Friends In The Life To Come,*" 1899, Warren & Son Printers and Publishers, London, pages 6 & 7.

Farrar, Frederic William

1831 – 1903, England. (Venerable Archdeacon Farrar, D.D., F.R.S.) A theological writer, born in Bombay, and educated at King Williams College, London University, University of Cambridge, and Marlborough College. He was Canon of Westminster and Rector of St. Margaret's, Archdeacon of Westminster, and Dean of Canterbury. It was by his theological works, however, that Farrar attained his greatest popularity.

"What then are the brutes that perish? Do they perish utterly and finally when something draws down their foreheads in the darkness and they die? Is a noble animal, which has almost risen to the virtues of humanity, less worthy to live than the man who in a thousand ways has debased himself below the level of the brutes?"

"This much at least has been seen and admitted by all philosophic theologians, that many of the arguments by which we maintain the immortality of man, are of nearly equal validity to maintain the immortality of our humbler kinsmen in the infinite graduations of the created world. So honest and profound a thinker as Bishop Butler was compelled to admit this in *Analogy of Natural and Revealed Religion.*"

Moor, J. Frewen, ***Thoughts Regarding The Future State Of Animals***, Quoted from a paper called *The Review of the Churches*, 1899, Warren & Son Printers and Publishers, London, pages 21 & 78.

Fuller, Andrew

1754 – 1815, England. Andrew Fuller is chiefly distinguished in connection with the foundation of the Baptist Missionary Society, to which he for most part devoted the energies of his life. He pastored two congregations in Soham and Kettering.

> "Sun, moon, stars, clouds, air, earth, sea, birds, beasts, fishes, and all other creatures which contributed to man's happiness, are through his revolt, in some way or other, made to subserve the cause of rebellion. To this 'vanity' they are subjected: 'not willingly' indeed; (for every creature in its proper station, naturally inclines to serve and honor its Creator, and whenever it does, otherwise, it is against nature) 'but by reason of him who hath subjected the same, in hope.'"
>
> "And as the 'redemption, or resurrection of our body' will mark the period when this disorder shall come to an end, it is considered as the birth-day of a new creation. Hence the interests of the sons of God are described as including those of creation in general. The latter are, as it were, bound up in the former: the glorious liberty of the one being a glorious liberty to the other, each longs for the same event – The earnest expectation of the creature waiteth for the manifestation of the sons of God."
>
> Fuller, Andrew, ***Dialogues, Letters, and Essays On Various Subjects***, 1810, Oliver D. Cooke, NY.

Fulton, John S.

1834 – 1907, Pennsylvania, New York. Rev. John S. Fulton, D.D., LL.D., D.C.L., was born in Scotland. He was educated at Aberdeen and came to the United States in 1850. He was Priest at New Orleans in 1857. Later he went to St. Louis where he became Rector of St. George's Protestant Episcopal Church. From St. Louis he came to New York and became

Editor of *The Church Standard*. Dr. Fulton was an Episcopal Clergyman noted as an able exponent of canon law, and Professor of that subject at the Episcopal Divinity School in Philadelphia. He is the author of several books.

Here is an excerpt of an article, which appeared in *The New York Times* dated November 19, 1899:

> "***On Kindness To Animals***: 'Kindness to animals, A Religious and Moral Duty' was the theme of an address delivered by Dr. John Fulton, Editor of *The Church Standard*, at the Church of the Ascension yesterday. Dr. Fulton held that kindness to animals was a religious duty. He said that countless millions of creatures go to make up the life of the universe, and it was inconceivable that there was no meaning in the life which the brute creation shared with mankind. He said that there was no argument in favor of the theory of continuous life for man that did not apply equally to a continuous life for the lower animals."
>
> Fulton, John S., *The New York Times*, ***On Kindness To Animals***, November 19, 1899.

Gurney, John Hampden

1802 – 1862, England. John Hampden Gurney, M.A., was an Anglican Clergyman and author of hymns. Educated at Trinity College, Cambridge, graduated with an MA. Curate of Lutterworth, Rector of St. Mary's Marylebone, and Prebendary of St. Paul's Cathedral.

> "The general strain of the passage seems to prepare us for something a little startling. If by 'creature' in the twentieth verse we understand the human family, it seems almost a truism to say that *they* were 'made subject to vanity.' It was hardly worthwhile for St. Paul to stop and explain his meaning, as he does in the twentieth verse, if he intended only to declare the well-known truth that man had fallen under the power of

evil, and had been enslaved by it from the beginning of time. Besides, he announces something, evidently, which he thinks will sound a little new when he says, in the next verse, that the 'creature itself shall be delivered one day from the bondage of corruption.'"

> Moor, J. Frewen, ***Thoughts Regarding The Future State Of Animals***, excerpt from Rev. J. Hampden Gurney's sermon on "*The Burdened Earth*," 1899, Warren & Son Printers and Publishers, London, page 88.

Hahne, Harry Alan

Arizona. Dr. Harry Hahne has been teaching courses in New Testament, Greek and computer-assisted Biblical research at several theological seminaries since 1986. He has been Associate Professor of New Testament Studies at Golden Gate Baptist Theological Seminary, Scottsdale, Arizona since 2002.

Prior to coming to Golden Gate, he taught for 16 years at Tyndale Seminary (formerly Ontario Theological Seminary). He has also taught courses at Heritage Baptist Seminary, Ontario Bible College and the University of Toronto, Wycliffe College. He has also served as a Pastor, a missionary, an electronic engineer and a software developer.

Dr. Hahne's Biblical studies research interests include the New Testament citations of the Old Testament, theology of nature, Pauline theology, the relationship between Second Temple Judaism and early Christianity, and computer-assisted Biblical research. He is the author of *The Corruption and Redemption of Creation: Nature in Romans 8.19-22 and Jewish Apocalyptic Literature* (T & T Clark), a book on the theology of nature in Jewish apocalyptic literature and the epistle to the Romans. He is assistant editor and a contributor to the Encyclopedia of Religion and Nature, and has published articles, various journals, and magazines.

Dr. Hahne has degrees in both Biblical studies and engineering. His doctorate is in Biblical studies from the University of Toronto (Wycliffe College). His doctoral dissertation compares the view of Jewish apocalyptic literature and Romans 8:19-22 concerning the corruption of the natural world due to sin, and its eschatological redemption.

> "Romans 8.19-22 is the most important passage expressing the Apostle Paul's theology of the present condition and eschatological hope of the natural world. The corruption and suffering of creation and its longing for deliverance are placed in the context of the suffering of the children of God, who look forward to sharing glory with Christ (vv. 17-30). The suffering of believers is part of the larger problem of the corruption of the entire created order, which was damaged by the fall of humanity. When the children of God are resurrected and enjoy eschatological glory with Christ, the whole creation will be transformed into a state of freedom and glory."
>
> Hahne, Harry Alan, *The Corruption And Redemption Of Creation: Nature in Romans 8.19-22 and Jewish Apocalyptic Literature*, 2006, T&T Clark, London, New York, page 1.

Haldane, Robert

1764 – 1842, Scotland. Rev. Robert Haldane was a Scottish churchman. He went to the University of Edinburgh where he studied divinity. He was licensed by the presbytery of Auchterarder, and then was appointed Minister at Drumelzier in Peeblesshire and was ordained in 1807. He was the principal of St. Mary's College and Professor of Theology, and Minister at the Holy Trinity Church in South Street, St. Andrews.

> "As the punishment of the sins of men is so much the greater as their effects extend to the creatures, in like

manner so much the greater will be the glory which shall be revealed in them, that the creatures which were formed for their use shall be made to participate with them in the day of the restitution of all things. Through the goodness of God they shall follow the deliverance and final destination of the children of God, and not that of His enemies."

"When God created the world, He saw 'everything that He had made, and behold it was very good.' When man transgressed, God viewed it a second time, and said, 'Cursed is the ground for thy sake.' The creature, then, has been subjected to the indignity which it now suffers in hope that it will one day be delivered from the bondage of corruption, and partake of the glorous freedom of the children of God. This hope was held out in the sentence pronounced on man, for in the doom of our first parents, the divine purpose of providing a deliverer was revealed. We know not the circumstances of this change, how it will be effected, or in what form the creation – those new Heavens and that new earth, wherein dwelleth righteousness, suited for the abode of the sons of God – shall then exist; but we are sure that it shall be worthy of the Divine wisdom, although at present beyond our comprehension."

> Moor, J. Frewen, ***Thoughts Regarding The Future State Of Animals***, An Exposition of the Epistle to the Romans by R. Haldane, Esq., *1899*, Warren & Son Printers and Publishers, London, page 109.

Hammond, Peter

1960 – South Africa. Rev. Dr. Peter Hammond is the Founder and Director of Frontline Fellowship, the Chairman of Africa Christian Action, the Director of the Christian Action Network, and the Chairman of the Reformation Society. He's been a pioneer missionary to Angola, Mozambique and Sudan, and the author of many books.

"A controversial question is whether it is God's plan for animals to be in Heaven or not. Many Christians believe that Heaven just would not be Heaven without animals. Certainly I believe that the Creator of millions of different species of animals, birds, insects and fish is a God who loves variety and prizes His creation. I cannot believe that Heaven will only be populated by angels and saints. From a careful study of the Bible I have become convinced that Heaven will be richer in vegetation and animal life than the most paradise-like part of earth could ever be. Where people get the idea of harps and clouds from, I don't know. God has a far greater plan than we can imagine."

"Wolves and sheep will live together in peace, and leopards will lie down with young goats, calves and lion cubs will feed together, and little children will take care of them. Cows and bears will eat together, and their calves and cubs will lie down in peace. Lions will eat straw as cattle do . . . The land will be as full of knowledge of the Lord as the seas are full of water." (Isaiah 11:6-9)

"'This plan, which God will complete when the time is right, is to bring all creation together, everything in Heaven and on earth, with Christ as head.' (Ephesians 1:10) 'Search in the Lord's book of living creatures and read what it says. Not one of these creatures will be missing and not one will be without its mate. The Lord has commanded it to be so; He Himself will bring them together. It is the Lord who will divide the land among them and give each of them a share. They will live in the land age after age, and it will belong to them for ever.'" (Isaiah 34:16, 17)

"When the revealed Word of God teaches us that God's eternal plan is for 'all creation' to be brought together under Christ then it includes all wildlife too. When God says 'everything,' He means everything – animals included."

"When He says that they will live for 'age after age,' 'forever,' this means eternal life. Only one place will last forever, and that is Heaven."

"That great book of worship in the Bible – the Psalms – reveals that all God's creation have contact with God (Psalm 93). All God's creatures praise Him. (Psalm 145:10). It is only mankind who needs forgiving and saving and teaching as to how to worship (Psalm 36 & 51), the animal kingdom worships God continually and naturally."

"Praise Him, hills and mountains, fruit trees and forests; all animals, tame and wild, reptiles and birds." (Psalm 148:9, 10)

"Be glad, earth and sky! Roar sea and every creature in you: be glad fields and everything in you! The trees in the woods will shout for joy." (Psalm 96:11, 12)

"The last book of the Bible presents the final climax of the ages when all creation faces the Creator. First the four living creatures (the animal-like angels around God's throne as described in Ezekiel) praise God, then the twenty-four elders, then the redeemed people of God, then the angels (Revelation 4:6 - 5:12), until finally the great scene is described when all living beings present their worship to Almighty God."

"And then I heard every creature in Heaven, on earth, in the world below, and in the sea – all living beings in the universe – and they were singing: To Him who sits on the throne and to the Lamb, be praise and honour, glory and might, forever and ever." (Revelation 5:13)

"In the light of these Scriptures, I firmly believe that our loving almighty Creator intends all His creatures to enjoy Heaven with Him forever. The only part of creation that will be missing from Heaven, according to the Bible, are those sinful human beings who neglect the great salvation that God has revealed in the Bible and provided through Christ. So while all the animal victims of scientific experiments will be in Heaven, the same cannot be said for all the hardhearted vivisectionists and ivory poachers."

>Hammond, Peter, *"The Bible And Animals,"*
>1984, Frontline Fellowship, South Africa,
>http://www.thebibleandanimals.org/.

"God's plan is to bring all creation together, everything in Heaven and earth, with Christ as head. Wolves and sheep will live together in peace, leopards will lie down with young goats, calves and lion cubs will feed together and little children will take care of them."

"There Is Eternal Life For Animals focuses on so many Scriptures which plainly deal with and include animals, showing that God does have a plan for animals, and just as Noah was commanded by God to provide for the saving of the animals from the flood, so Christians can expect Christ's much greater redemption to include all the incredibly diverse animals which the Lord has created."

>Letter to Niki Behrikis Shanahan reviewing
>*There Is Eternal Life For Animals,* June 19, 2003.

Headlam, Arthur Cayley

1862 – 1947, England. Rev. A. C. Headlam, B.D., was an English Theologian, and Anglican Bishop of Gloucester from 1923 to 1945. He was educated at Winchester College and New College, Oxford. He was a Fellow of All Souls College,

Oxford in 1885. He was ordained in 1888, and became Rector of Welwyn in 1896. Rev. Headlam was Regius Professor of Divinity, Oxford from 1918 to 1923. He was influential in the Church of England's council on foreign relations in the 1930s, chairing the Committee on Relations with Episcopal Churches. He supported the Protestant Reich Church in Germany, and was a critic of the Confessing Church. The historian, James Wycliffe Headlam, was his brother.

> "(Romans 8:18-25) What though the path to that glory lies through suffering? The suffering and the glory alike are parts of a great cosmical movement, in which the irrational creation joins with man. As it shared the results of his fall, so also will it share in his redemption. Its pangs are pangs of a new birth. Like the mute creation, we Christians, too, wait painfully for our deliverance. Our attitude is one of hope and not of possession."

> "What of that? For the sufferings which we have to undergo in this phase of our career I count not worth a thought in view of that dazzling splendor which will one day break through the clouds and dawn upon us. For the songs of God will stand forth revealed in the glories of their bright inheritance. And for that consummation not they alone but the whole irrational creation, both animate and inanimate, waits with eager longing; like spectators straining forward over the ropes to catch the first glimpse of some triumphal pageant."

> "The future and not the present must satisfy its aspirations. For ages ago Creation was condemned to have its energies marred and frustrated. And that by no act of its own: it was God who fixed this doom upon it, but with the hope that as it had been enthralled to death and decay by the Fall of Man so, too, the Creation shall share in the free and glorious existence of God's emancipated children. It is like the pangs of a woman in childbirth. This universal frame feels up to this

moment the throes of travail – feels them in every part and cries out in its pain. But where there is travail, there must needs also be a birth."

"In fact, it is nothing short of an universal law that suffering marks the road to glory. All the suffering, and all the imperfection, all the unsatisfied aspiration and longing of which the traces are so abundant in external nature as well as in man, do but point forward to a time when the suffering shall cease, the imperfection be removed and the frustrated aspirations at last crowned and satisfied; and this time coincides with the glorious consummation which awaits the Christian."

"True it is that there goes up as it were an universal groan, from creation, from ourselves, from the Holy Spirit who sympathizes with us; but this groaning is but the travail-pangs, of the new birth, the entrance upon their glorified condition of the risen sons of God."

> Headlam, Arthur Cayley; Sanday, William, *The International Critical Commentary on the Holy Scriptures of the Old and New Testaments, The Epistle To The Romans,* 1896, Charles Scribner's Sons, New York, pages 204-206.

Henry, Matthew

1662 – 1714, England. English Clergyman and Bible Commentator. Minister of a Presbyterian congregation at Chester. Henry is well-known for his Exposition of the Old and New Testaments (1708-1710).

An excerpt from Matthew Henry's commentary on Romans.

"And this redemption of the creature is reserved till then; for, as it was with man and for man that they fell under the curse, so with man and for man they shall be delivered. All the curse and filth that now adhere to the creature shall be done away then when those that have suffered with Christ upon earth shall reign with Him upon the earth. This the whole creation looks and longs for; and it may serve as a reason why now a good man should be merciful to his beast."

> Henry, Matthew, ***Commentary of the Whole Bible Volume VI (Acts to Revelation), Romans***, Christian Classics Ethereal Library, Calvin College, Michigan, www.ccel.org.

An excerpt from Matthew Henry's commentary on Proverbs.

"He regards even the life of his beast, not only because it is his servant, but because it is God's creature, and in conformity to Providence, which *preserves man and beast*. (Psalm 36:6) The beasts that are under our care must be provided for, must have convenient food and rest, must in no case be abused or tyrannized over. Balaam was checked for beating his ass. The law took care for oxen. Those therefore are unrighteous men that are not just to the brute-creatures; those that are furious and barbarous to them evidence, and confirm in themselves, a habit of barbarity, and help to make the creation groan."

> Henry, Matthew, ***Commentary on the Whole Bible Volume III (Job to Song of Solomon), Proverbs***, Christian Classics Ethereal Library, Calvin College, Michigan, www.ccel.org.

Hitchcock, Edward

1793 – 1864, Massachusetts. Rev. Hitchcock was the third President of Amherst College, Amherst, Massachusetts. He was a geologist and was a congregational Pastor. A few years later he left the ministry to become Professor of Chemistry and Natural History at Amherst College.

"The passage in Psalms, which says: "Man that is in honor and abideth not, is like the beasts that perish," cannot mean that they will never live again, for that would be to say the same of men, who are here said to be 'like' them in this behalf. The great German Theologian, Tholuck, is of the same opinion, as was also Martin Luther."

>Moor, J. Frewen, ***Thoughts Regarding The Future State Of Animals***, Religion of Geology by Dr. Hitchcock, 1899, Warren & Son Printers and Publishers, London, page 13.

Hoffman, Frank L.

1939 – New York. Rev. Frank Hoffman is a retired Jewish-United Methodist Pastor. He and his wife, Mary, are the founders of The Mary T. and Frank L. Hoffman Family Foundation. http://all-creatures.org

>"It is amazing how many Scriptures plainly proclaim the truth about the whole of creation. Over a hundred Scriptures (not only the two or three witnesses necessary for confirmation of a question or statement, as we are taught in the Bible) show that God has a plan for the animals."

>Review letter to Niki Behrikis Shanahan for ***There Is Eternal Life For Animals.***

Johnson, Barton W.

1833 – 1894, Illinois. Johnson attended Eureka College and Bethany College. He took a position in Eureka College, where he remained for seven years, two of which as its President. He acted as corresponding and financial secretary of the American Missionary Society. He accepted the Presidency of Oskaloosa College in connection with the care of the Church at Oskaloosa. He became editor of *The Evangelist*. He wrote several books, such as, *The Vision of the Ages, Commentary of*

John, The People's New Testament, and *Christian Lesson Commentary.*

> "The whole world is represented earnestly looking forward to that day of future glory when the sons of God will have reached their high estate and be revealed as His children. It is a fine, poetic figure, a grand conception. For the creature was made subject to vanity. The *creation* was subjected to vanity; *i. e.,* became empty; lost its original significance. The Greek word rendered 'vanity,' means 'to seek without finding.' God placed 'the creation' under man's dominion, and when man fell the whole was subject to vanity by God. In hope – a hope was left to creation in its fallen estate. A promise of final redemption was made to fallen man (Genesis 3:15), and the creation is represented as sharing that hope."
>
> Johnson, Barton W., ***The People's New Testament***, *Commentary of Romans*, 1891.

Josephus, Flavius

c. 37 – c. 100 AD/CE, Born in Jerusalem. Josephus was a 1st century Jewish historian and apologist of priestly and royal ancestry who survived and recorded the Destruction of Jerusalem in 70. His works give an important insight into first-century Judaism. Josephus offers information about individuals, groups, customs, and geographical places.

> "There will be no more generations of wild beasts, nor will the substance of the rest of the animals shoot out any more; for it will not produce men, but the number of the righteous will continue, and never fail, together with righteous angels, and spirits [of God], and with His word, as a choir of righteous men and women that never grow old, and continue in an incorruptible state, singing hymns to God, who hath advanced them to that happiness, by the means of a regular institution of life;

with whom the whole creation also will lift up a perpetual hymn from *corruption, to incorruption,* as glorified by a splendid and pure spirit. It will not then be restrained by a bond of necessity, but with a lively freedom shall offer up a voluntary hymn, and shall praise Him that made them, together with the angels, and spirits, and men now *freed from all bondage."*

> Josephus, Flavius, **Discourse To The Greeks Concerning Hades**, Christian Classics Ethereal Library, Calvin College, Michigan, www.ccel.org.

In his writings called *The Antiquities Of The Jews*, Josephus makes the statement that "all the living creatures had one language." He indicates that in the Garden of Eden, Adam and Eve communicated in the same language as all the animals. Josephus tells us that the lines of communication changed after Adam and Eve sinned.

Keble, John

1792 – 1866, England. Rev. John Keble was Vicar of Coln St. Aldwyn's. He became a fellow of Oriel College, Oxford, and was for some years a tutor and examiner in the University. While still at Oxford he took Holy Orders in 1815. In 1835 he was appointed Vicar of Hursley, Hampshire, where he settled down to family life and remained for the rest of his life as a parish priest at All Soul's Church.

> "Mr. Keble speaks of the meanest things below as sharing in the blessings of redemption, and looking forward to the 'return' of God at the last for the full enjoyment of these blessings."
>
> It was not then a poet's dream, An idle vaunt of song,
> Which bids us hear, at each sweet pause
> From care, and want, and toil,
> When dewy eve her curtain draws
> Over the day's turmoil, In the low chant of wakeful birds,

In the deep weltering flood,
In whispering leaves, these solemn words:
"God made us all for good." All true, all faultless, all in tune,
Creation's wondrous choir
Open'd in mystic unison, To last till time expire.
The travail pains of earth must last
Till her appointed time.
The hour that saw from opening Heaven
Redeeming glory stream,
Beyond the summer hues of even,
Beyond the mid-day beam.
Thenceforth, to eyes of high desire,
The meanest things below, As with a seraph's robe of fire
Invested, burn and glow.
The rod of Heaven has touched them all,
The word from Heaven is spoken:
"Rise, shine, and sing thou captive thrall;
"Are not they fetters broken?
The God Who hallowed thee and blest,
Pronouncing thee all good –
Hath He not all thy wrongs redrest,
And all thy bliss renewed?
"Why mourn'st thou still as one bereft,
Now that the eternal Son
His blessed home in Heaven hath left
To make thee all His own?"
Thou mourn'st because sin lingers still
In Christ's new Heaven and earth;
Because our rebel works and will
Stain our immortal birth:
Hence all thy groans and travail pains,
Hence, till thy God return,
In wisdom's ear thy blithest strains,
Oh! Nature, seem to mourn.

John Keble

Moor, J. Frewen, ***Thoughts Regarding The Future State Of Animals***, *The Christian Year*, 1899, Warren & Son Printers and Publishers, London, Reference to *The Christian Year,* Oxford, 1827, pages 9-11.

Kirby, H.

Canada. Rev. H. Kirby was an Anglican Minister at Harbour Grace, Canada.

"To this conclusion Holy Scripture very clearly points in the Epistle to the Romans, where we are told that not only mankind, but the whole creation, are led by God to look forward to some alleviation of their present bondage, which shall be the result of the Incarnation of God the Son."

Moor, J. Frewen, ***Thoughts Regarding The Future State Of Animals***, article from *Animal World* by Rev. H. Kirby, 1880, 1899, Warren & Son Printers and Publishers, London, Reference to *The Christian Year,* Oxford, 1827, page 56.

Lindsay, James Gordon

1906 – 1973, Illinois, Texas (Gordon Lindsay). Evangelist, Pastor, and author. At the age of 18 Lindsay began his ministry as a traveling evangelist conducting meetings in Assembly of God churches and other Pentecostal groups. He was the Pastor of a church in Ashland, Oregon. He became William Branham's manager in 1947. He sponsored mission programs in several foreign countries, and started a radio ministry. Lindsay was a prolific writer, publishing over 250 volumes of doctrinal books. Rev. Gordon Lindsay was the Founder of Christ For The Nations Institute, Texas, in 1970.

In a book by Gordon Lindsay called ***Difficult Questions About The Bible Answered,*** he says that animals have souls, and that apparently there will be a regeneration and restoration of the animals.

Lloyd-Jones, D. Martyn

1899 – 1981, Wales and England. (David Martyn Lloyd-Jones) A Protestant Christian Minister who was hugely influential in the reformed wing of the British evangelical movement in the 20th century. For almost 30 years, he was the Minister of Westminster Chapel in London.

In his book ***Romans: The Final Perseverance of the Saints.*** Lloyd-Jones discusses the meaning of Romans 8:18-23 relative to who "creation" or "the creature" is. He says it means animals, and the rest of nature, and that the Apostle Paul is saying they are earnestly expecting and waiting for this great event along with the sons of God.

Luther, Martin

1483 – 1546, Germany. A German monk, priest, professor, theologian, and church reformer. His teachings inspired the Reformation and deeply influenced the doctrines, and culture of the Lutheran and Protestant traditions, as well as the course of Western civilization.

Martin Luther's life and work influenced the development of western culture in other ways, as well. His translation of the Bible furthered the development of a standard version of the German language, and added several principles to the art of translation. His translation significantly influenced the English King James Version of the Bible. Due to the recently developed printing press, his writings were widely read, influencing many subsequent Protestant Reformers and thinkers, giving rise to diversifying Protestant traditions in Europe and elsewhere. Luther's hymns, including his best-known "***A Mighty Fortress Is Our God***," inspired the development of congregational singing within Christianity.

Martin Luther says in his commentary on I Timothy that God preserves all things from death – even beasts. He refers to Psalms 36:6 which says "Thy righteousness is like the great mountains; thy judgments are a great deep: O Lord, thou preservest man and beast."

> "Our Lord has written the promise of the resurrection not in books alone, but in every leaf in the springtime."
> Martin Luther

MacDonald, George

1824 – 1905, Scotland. George MacDonald was a Scottish author, poet, and Christian Minister. He took his degree at the University of Aberdeen, and then went to London, studying at Highbury College for the Congregational ministry. In 1850 he was appointed Pastor of Trinity Congregational Church, Arundel. He later settled in London and taught for some time at the University of London.

George Macdonald wrote ***The Hope Of The Gospel*** in 1892. This is such a good book, that I think any animal lover would like to read it. I had a hard time deciding which passages to use, because there are so many good sections of the book. It is free to read online at www.gutenberg.org, but you may wish to buy a hard copy for convenience. Here are some excerpts from the chapter called *The Hope Of The Universe.*

> "Note now 'the hope that the creation itself also,' as something besides and other than God's men and women, 'shall be delivered from the bondage of corruption, into the liberty of the glory of the children of God.' The creation then is to share in the deliverance and liberty and glory of the children of God. Deliverance from corruption, liberty from bondage, must include escape from the very home and goal of corruption, namely death, – and that in all its kinds and degrees. When you say then that for the children of God there is no more death, remember that

the deliverance of the creature is from the bondage of corruption into the glorious liberty of the children of God. Dead, in bondage to corruption, how can they share in the liberty of the children of life? Where is their deliverance?"

"What lovelier feature in the newness of the new earth, than the old animals glorified with us, in their home with us — our common home, the house of our father — each kind an unfailing pleasure to the other! Ah, what horses! Ah, what dogs! Ah, what wild beasts, and what birds in the air! The whole redeemed creation goes to make up St. Paul's Heaven. He had learned of Him who would leave no one out; who made the excuse for his murderers that they did not know what they were doing."

"Is not the prophecy on the groaning creation to have its fulfillment in the new Heavens and the new earth, wherein dwelleth righteousness? Does not this involve its existence beyond what we call this world? Why should it not then involve immortality? Would it not be more like the king eternal, immortal, invisible, to know no life but the immortal? To create nothing that could die; to slay nothing but evil? 'For He is not a God of the dead, but of the living; for all live unto Him.'"

"'And not only so' – that the creation groaneth and travaileth – 'but ourselves also, which have the first fruits of the spirit, even we ourselves groan within ourselves, waiting for .... the redemption of our body.' – We are not free, he implies, until our body is redeemed; then all the creation will be free with us. He regards the creation as part of our embodiment. The whole creation is waiting for the manifestation of the sons of God – that is, the redemption of their body, the idea of which extends to their whole material envelopment, with all the life that belongs to it. For this as for them, the bonds of corruption must fall away; it must enter into the same liberty with them, and be that for which it was created – a vital temple, perfected by the unbroken indwelling of its divinity."

MacDonald, George, *The Hope Of The Gospel*, 1892, www.gutenberg.org, Utah.

Main, William

England. The following is a quote by Rev. W. Main of Perth, England, from "*Man's dominion over the creatures, its nature and limits.*"

"Through the sanctification of man, the animals shall be restored to that sympathy with him and their rightful place in his dominion which his own sin has destroyed. Brethren, we hope and pray for that time to be realized when the full sanctification and highest blessedness of humanity shall be consummated – for God is faithful, Who has promised. But in our hopes and prayers let us not forget the lower animals, who will proportionately rise with us, as we ourselves are exalted."

Moor, J. Frewen, *Thoughts Regarding The Future State Of Animals*, from a sermon by Rev. W. Main, "*Man's dominion over the creatures, its nature and limits,*" 1899, Warren & Son Printers & Publishers, London, page 99.

Marvin, Frederic Rowland

1847 – 1919, New York. Clergyman and author. Attended Lafayette College, PA, graduated College of Physicians & Surgeons, M.D. and the Seminary of the Reformed Church in America, NJ; ordained 1879. Pastor of the congregational church at Middletown, NY, and Great Barrington, MA.

The following is a quote from the book, ***Christ Among The Cattle***, A Sermon preached in The First Congregational Church, Portland, Oregon.

"There is nothing in the Bible, when rightly understood, to discountenance the belief that both man and beast enter upon a future life when the joys and sorrows of this life have ended."

"It is an important part of a good man's religion to be kind to the animal world, and it is literally true that – "

> He prayeth well who loveth well
> Both man and bird and beast.
> He prayeth best who loveth best
> All things, both great and small,
> For the dear God who loveth us
> He made and loveth all.
>
> Samuel Taylor Coleridge

"I am sincerely happy to find that I am not the only believer in the immortality of the animals. The longer I live the more convinced I am that we all – men, beasts, birds, fishes and insects – are the creatures of a loving God, who will not allow a sparrow to fall to the earth without His notice."

Marvin, Frederic Rowland, ***Christ Among The Cattle***, 1912, Sherman, French & Company, Boston, pages 25-26 and 55-56.

McGee, J. Vernon

1904 – 1988, Texas. (John Vernon McGee, Th.D., LL.D.) John Vernon McGee graduated with his B. Div. from Columbia Theological Seminary and his Th.M. and Th.D. from Dallas Theological Seminary in Dallas. He served Presbyterian churches in Georgia, Tennessee, and Texas. He Pastored the Lincoln Avenue Presbyterian Church in Pasadena, California, and Pastored the Church of the Open Door from 1949 to 1970. In 1967 he began the "Thru the Bible Radio Network" program.

In his Thru The Bible Commentary series of Romans, Chapters 1-8, J. Vernon McGee tells about "The New Creation" and says that not only the bodies of believers are to be redeemed, but the entire physical universe, this earth is to be redeemed.

In his Thru The Bible Commentary series of Revelation, Chapters 1-5 McGee states that these living creatures also represent the animal world, as suggested by Godet. The lion represents wild beasts, the calf represents domesticated beasts, the eagle represents birds, and man is the head of all creation. Here is the Bible verse he is referring to: "And the first beast was like a lion, and the second beast like a calf, and the third beast had a face as a man, and the fourth beast was like a flying eagle." (Revelation 7, KJV)

Moor, John Frewen

1823 – 1906, England. John Frewen Moor, M.A. graduated at Oriel College, Oxford. He became Vicar of Ampfield in 1853. Rev. Moor is the author of the book ***Thoughts Regarding The Future State Of Animals.***

> Kind reader, now I've done my task,
> Two things of you I dare to ask:
> Make love within your heart to glow,
> To all around your kindness show.
> May we enjoy in realms above
> The blessings of eternal love:
> When man released from pain and care,
> With bird and beast shall Heaven share.
> Man, beast, and bird, yea creatures all,
> No longer cursed for man's sad fall,
> In chorus joined shall voices raise,
> To sing their loved Creator's praise.
>
> John Frewen Moor

Moor, J. Frewen, ***Thoughts Regarding The Future State Of Animals***, 1899, Warren & Son Printers and Publishers, London, page 183.

Moorehead, William Gallogly

1836 – 1914, Ohio. William Gallogly Moorehead, D.D., LL.D., was Professor of New Testament literature and exegesis. President of the faculty in Xenia Theological Seminary, Ohio. Educated at Allegheny Theological Seminary and Xenia Theological Seminary. He was ordained in 1862. Missionary of the American and Foreign Christian Union, Italy, 1862-69. Pastor of First United Presbyterian church, Xenia in 1870. Editor of the Scofield Reference Bible. Served on the Board of Trustees, Lincoln University and Theological Seminary. Author of ***Outline Studies In The Books Of The Old Testament, Studies In The Mosaic Institutions, Studies In The Four Gospels, Outline Studies In Acts — Ephesians, Outline Studies In Philippians — Hebrew, A Help To The Study Of The Holy Spirit,*** and ***Studies In The Book Of Revelation.***

> "What a crowning day that will be when the sons shall be conformed to the likeness of the Son of God, shall sparkle in the radiance of His effulgent glory. And they shall 'sit with Me in My throne' (Rev. 3:21). 'For whom He did foreknow He also did predestinate to be conformed to the image of His Son, that He might be the firstborn among many brethren' (v. 29). Such is the destiny in store for the children and heirs of God. The perfect archetype according to which they are to be fashioned is the glorified Christ (Phil. 3:20, 21). In the grace and love of their Lord they are already sons, and kings, and priests."

> "While they are in the world there is no hint of such indescribable destiny. Here they are pilgrims and strangers; are surrounded by a suffering creation, are

compassed with infirmities and weaknesses, are hedged in by countless limitations, bemoan their failures and confess their sins. How little they look like God's heirs, God's kings and priests! 'The whole creation groaneth and travaileth in pain together until now. And not only so, but we ourselves, who have the firstfruits of the Spirit, even we ourselves groan within ourselves, waiting.' It is a wondrous picture, and of course perfectly true. Nature groans. All her cries and sounds are in the minor key. The voices of most of the animals are keyed to minor strains. The winds and the waves sigh and moan. Striking are the words of Jeremiah, 'There is sorrow on the sea; it cannot be quiet.' Our groans are in unison and sympathy with a groaning creation. 'An absent King, a present usurper, a cursed soil, overflowing evil, disease, sorrow, death' – surely there is enough to make us groan."

"But creation waits, as do all who believe. 'For the earnest expectation of the creation waiteth for the revealing of the sons of God.' Her eagerness is expressed by vivid terms, the head bent forward, and the neck outstretched. 'Her out-looking face is an off-looking face, turned from every direction but one.' Her waiting is watching, and her watching is waiting, and both are in hope of deliverance from the bondage of corruption into the liberty of the glory of the children of God. The heirs travel incognito, as many a prince has done."

"By and by the disguise shall drop off, and they shall be like Christ Himself, for they shall see Him as He is. When that blessed day comes, as come it must, the planet itself shall share in the glory, and 'Paradise Lost' shall be succeeded by 'Paradise Regained.' In view of this matchless future awaiting the children of God and creation also, Paul's word should ever be in our hearts if not on our lips, 'For I reckon that the sufferings of this present time are not worthy to be compared with the glory which shall be revealed in us.' The saint's everlasting inheritance – who can compute its value, or measure its greatness?"

> Moorehead, William G., ***Outline Studies In Acts, Romans, First And Second Corinthians, Galatians And Ephesians***, 1902, Fleming H. Revell Company, Chicago, New York, Toronto.

Morris, Francis Orpen

1810 – 1893, England. He graduated at Worcester College, Oxford in 1833, and was ordained in 1834, He became Rector of Nunburnholine, Yorkshire since 1854. Morris became an early advocate for conservation, and was instrumental in founding The Royal Society for the Protection of Birds.

> "'Thou Lord shalt save both man and beast.' (Psalm 36:6) It seems to me hardly possible that any one could be cruel to an animal if he believed in the future existence of that creature after death. It is most likely that very few persons of those here present have ever thought of such a thing. The idea of it is now put before you, and I imagine that many would be at first disposed to deny the possibility, and many more the probability of it, but certainly it is not impossible. On the contrary, it is probable, and there is good reason to believe that it is so. It was the opinion, among those of many others, of the great Bishop Butler, one of the most profound thinkers that ever lived. He wrote, 'We cannot argue from the reason of the thing that death is the destruction of living agents. Neither can we find anything in the whole analogy of nature to afford us even the slightest presumption that animals ever lose their living powers; much less, if it were possible, that they lose them by death.' He adds: 'All difficulties to the contrary are so apparently and wholly founded in

our ignorance, that it is wonderful they should be insisted on by any but such as are weak enough to think that they are acquainted with the whole system of things.'"

> Moor, J. Frewen, ***Thoughts Regarding The Future State Of Animals***, from a sermon by Rev. F. O. Morris entitled "*The Curse of Cruelty*" preached in York Minster on May 9, 1886, 1899, Warren & Son Printers and Publishers, London, page 11.

Newell, William Reed

1868 – 1956, Ohio, Illinois. William Reed Newell attended Wooster College in Ohio and graduated in 1891. After studies at Princeton and Oberlin Seminaries, he Pastored the Bethesda Congregational Church in Chicago until 1895, when Moody invited him to become the Assistant Superintendent of Moody Bible Institute under R. A. Torrey. He wrote the famous hymn, *At Calvary*.

> "Let us note that the Spirit does not take us out of sympathy with groaning creation, but rather supports us in such sympathy! Being ourselves, as to the body, in a groaning condition, —'longing to be clothed upon with our house which is from Heaven' (II Cor. 5:2) we are able to sympathize with the creatures about us, which is a precious thing! No one should feel as tender as should the child of God toward suffering creation. No one should be as gentle. Not only should this be true about us as concerns unsaved people: as Paul says, 'Be gentle, showing all meekness toward all *men*,' but, I say, we should be tender and patient toward animals, for they are in a dying state — until our bodies are redeemed."

> "Thus, then, does the Christian become the true connection of groaning creation with God! He is

redeemed, Heavenly; but his body is unredeemed, earthly. Yet the blessed Holy Spirit as the "firstfruits" of coming bodily redemption, dwells in him. Thus the believer and the whole creation look toward one goal – the liberty of the coming glory of the sons of God!"

>Newell, William R., ***Romans Verse-By-Verse***, Christian Classics Ethereal Library, Calvin College, Michigan, www.ccel.org.

Pettingill, William Leroy

1886 – 1950, Delaware, Philadelphia, New York. A prolific writer of numerous books, preacher, and one of the consulting editors of the *Scofield Reference Bible*. He co-founded The Philadelphia School of the Bible with C. I. Scofield in 1913, and served as Dean until 1928. He was ordained by the National Baptist Convention in 1899, and became Pastor of North Church in Wilmington, Delaware. He founded two periodicals, *Serving and Waiting* (1911) and *Just A Word* (1928), both devoted to fundamentalist and dispensationalist ideas. In 1948 Pettingill accepted the call to Pastor the First Baptist Church in New York City.

>"'For the creation was subjected to vanity' (20, 21, R.V.). Upon this complicated passage we quote Dr. Stifler at length: 'As God's sons look with longing to the future, first, because their present condition is painful and is not the ideal condition, and secondly, because the future will bring them redemption, just so the creation, personified all through this passage, looks to the same future, first, because it is now under the curse, and, secondly, in the future, in the glorification of the faithful, it will find deliverance. The 20th verse gives a reason for the 'earnest expectation' drawn from the present condition of creation, and the next verse a reason (when we read 'because') drawn from the future. 'Was made subject to vanity' is ambiguous.

Creation was not made so, for originally creation was 'good,' and it was subjected to vanity, that is, to attain to no good end permanently."

"Any good that comes from creation must be evoked by man's toil. This condition did not come about by its own ('willingly'), but because of Him (God) Who subjected it to vanity, not finally, but upon a basis of some provision for the future, called 'hope.' This verse clearly implies that creation ('all nature') is neither in its original condition nor in its final condition. It fell when man fell (Genesis 3:17-19); it shall be restored when he is, and shall be no longer subject to vanity, but to him (Heb. 2:5-9). It is eagerly awaiting the revelation of God's sons, because that is the time when it 'also shall be delivered from the bondage of corruption (the subjection, v. 20) into the liberty of the glory ('glorious liberty' is wrong) of the children of God.' The creation is promised the liberty of the glory, not the glory."

> Pettingill, William Leroy, *Simple Studies In Romans*, 1915, Philadelphia School of the Bible, Pennsylvania, pages 110-111.

Phillips, Forbes Alexander

1866 – 1917, England. (Pseudonym Athol Forbes) Vicar of Gorleston, Great Yarmouth; Rector of Southtown; novelist, and dramatist. Durham University and private tutors. Ordained to All Saints' in Newcastle, 1889; Senior Curate to Tynemouth Parish Church, 1891-1893; Vicar and Rector, Gorleston, 1893; surrogate for Norfolk and Suffolk, 1894. Select speaker Church Congress, 1895; past provincial Grand Chaplain of Norfolk and Suffolk; prelate of the Order of Knights Templar; Plantagenet preceptory. He was Chaplain to Church Actors' Union; Chaplain, V Norfolk Territorial.

Here are excerpts from an article in *The London Daily Mail*, 1898, ProQuest Historical Newspapers, *The New York Times*.

Newspaper Headline: ***"Athol Forbes" On Animals.***

Newspaper Subtitle: *"The English Vicar Who Firmly Believes in Their Immortality – The Bible Quoted in Support."*

"The remarks recently made in the pulpit by the Rev. Forbes Phillips, ('Athol Forbes') Vicar of Gorleston, Yarmouth, and reported in the *Daily Mail*, to the effect that he believed animals had a future existence, and that he would rather meet in Heaven some animals than some people he had met on earth, continue to bring in to him a large number of letters on the subject."

"I shall never forget the look of alarm and astonishment on the faces of some members of the congregation when I happened once to express in the pulpit my belief in their future life."

"The truth is, the men who wrote the Bible no more doubted the future existence of their beasts than they did their own. Job speaks of the spirit of the man and the spirit of the beast."

Phillips, Forbes Alexander, ***Athol Forbes On Animals,*** 1898, *The London Daily Mail.*

Pringle, William

1790 – 1860, England. Rev. William Pringle translated some of Hermann Witsius and John Calvin's commentaries in the mid-19th century. University of Edinburgh, University in Glasgow, Burgher Divinity Hall at Selkirk. He was ordained in 1819. The College of New Jersey, Princeton conferred the Doctor of Divinity upon the Rev. William Pringle.

"But if we refer to the Scriptures, the very text before us is sufficient to settle the matter; for how can it be said that they are earnestly expecting their deliverance along with the sons of God, if there is to be no future state of existence for them? The Scriptures having been written for man's learning, there is consequently little said of the provision that is made for the futurity of the animals; and yet there is sufficient said to prove, that, the Judge of all earth will show no partiality, and will not overlook the meanest of His works."

> Moor, J. Frewen, ***Thoughts Regarding The Future State Of Animals,*** extract from a tract written by W. Pringle entitled "*Some Reflections on the Present and Future Condition of the Animal Tribes,*" 1899, Warren & Son Printers and Publishers, London, page 18.

Pusey, Edward Bouverie

1800 – 1882, England. An English churchman and Regius Professor of Hebrew at Christ Church, Oxford. He was one of the leaders of the Oxford Movement. After attending Eton College, Edward became a commoner of Christ Church, and was elected in 1824 to a fellowship at Oriel College. Between 1825 and 1827, he studied Oriental languages and German theology at the University of Gottingen. In 1828 the Prime Minister, the Duke of Wellington, appointed him to the Regius Professorship of Hebrew with the attached canonry of Christ Church.

> "In his 'Parochial Sermons,' the sober-minded Dr. Pusey says that 'all nature, having suffered together, shall be restored together. Things animate and inanimate, as being the works of God, bear in themselves some likeness to their Maker, and traces of His hands. As, then, to us death is to be the gate of immortality and glory, so in some way to them … Creation includes all created beings … All creation must include our nature too, in that one common groan and pang.'"

Pusey, Edward Bouverie, ***Our Animal Friends*** (A Monthly Magazine published by The American Society for the Prevention of Cruelty to Animals), 1893, New York.

Pym, William Wollaston

1792 – 1852, England. Rev. William Wollaston Pym was the Rector and Vicar of Willian, Hertfordshire, England.

> "By 'the creature' I can only understand the subordinate creation, called 'the whole creation,' which, at the first, was made 'very good,' but which was cursed for the sin of man, as was the very earth upon which he trod: God thereby exhibiting His abhorrence of man's rebellion against Himself. St. Paul, considering how the creature had groaned under the effects of sin, and its consequent curse, for more than four thousand years, represents the suffering part of God's creation as longing for deliverance from the yoke of vanity to which it was thus subjected, and links the season of its deliverance with 'the manifestation of the sons of God.'"

> "The restitution of all things, therefore, in this earth, we understand to mean, that almighty act whereby everything, which has been cursed for the sin of man, shall be restored to at least its primitive state of perfection and blessing, though, we conceive, to a higher degree." (*And He shall send Jesus Christ, which before was preached unto you: Whom the Heaven must receive until the times of restitution of all things, which God hath spoken by the mouth of all His holy prophets since the world began. Acts 3:20-21*)

Pym, William Wollaston, ***The Restitution Of All Things***, 1843, James Nisbet & Co., London.

Sanday, William

1843 – 1920, England. Rev. William Sanday, D.D., LL.D. was a British Theologian and Biblical Scholar. Professor of Exegesis at Oxford between 1883 and 1895, as well as Lady Margaret Professor of Divinity and Canon of Christ Church between 1895 and 1919. He also worked as one of the editors of the 1880 Variorum Bible.

Please see entry above under "Headlam," coauthor with Sanday of *The Epistle of Romans*.

> Headlam, Arthur Cayley; Sanday, William, *The International Critical Commentary on the Holy Scriptures of the Old and New Testaments, The Epistle To The Romans*, 1896, Charles Scribner's Sons, New York.

Scott, Thomas

1747 – 1821, England. English Clergyman and Biblical Scholar. He is principally known for his best-selling work *A Commentary On The Whole Bible*, and as one of the founders of the Church Missionary Society. He was hospital Chaplain at the Lock Hospital in London, and became Rector of Aston Sandford in Buckinghamshire where he remained until his death.

> "The whole visible creation seems to *wait* with earnest expectation, for that important period, when the *children of God* shall be manifested in the glory which is prepared for them ... Everything seems perverted from its intended use: the inanimate creatures were pressed into the service of man's rebellion ... The animal tribes are subject to pain and death through man's sin; and their sufferings are exceedingly increased by his cruelty, who instead of a kind master is become their inhuman butcher and tyrant ... so that every thing is in an unnatural state; the *good* creatures

of God *appear evil* through man's abuse of them, and even the enjoyment originally to be found in them, is turned into vexation, bitterness, and disappointment ... yet this otherwise most deplorable state of the creation, is *in hope*: God intends to rescue it from this confused state, and to deliver it from being thus *held in bondage* to man's depravity, that it may partake of *the glorious liberty* of His children, and minister to it."

    Moor, J. Frewen, ***Thoughts Regarding The Future State Of Animals,*** extract from Scott's Commentary on Romans 8:18-23, 1899, Warren & Son Printers & Publishers, London, page 94.

Stott, John Robert Walmsley

1921 – England. British Christian leader and Anglican Clergyman who is noted as a leader of the worldwide evangelical movement. Scott studied modern languages at Trinity College, Cambridge, where he graduated with a double first in French and Theology. Then he transferred to Ridley Hall Theological College (also of the University of Cambridge) so he could become ordained as an Anglican Vicar. He was ordained in 1945 and went on to become a Curate at the Church of All Souls, Langham Place from 1945-1950, then as Rector from 1950-75, and as Rector Emeritus since 1975. He was appointed a Chaplain to Elizabeth II of the United Kingdom (1959-1991), and an Extra Chaplain in 1991. He received a CBE in the new years honors list, 2006.

He has written over 40 books, and he founded the Langham Partnership International (known as John Stott Ministries in the U.S.) in 1974, and the London Institute for Contemporary Christianity in 1982 of which he is now the honorary president.

Scott is an avid birder, and has taken numerous trips in many different countries to observe and study birds, as well as writing a book about them entitled, *The Birds Our Teachers: Biblical Lessons from a Lifelong Bird Watcher.*

In a November 2004 editorial on Stott, *New York Times* columnist David Brooks cited Michael Cromartie of the Ethics and Public Policy Center as saying that "if evangelicals could elect a pope, Stott is the person they would likely choose."

> "The sufferings and the glory concern both God's creation and God's children. Paul now writes from a cosmic perspective. The sufferings and glory of the old creation (the material order) and of the new (the people of God) are integrally related to each other. Both creations are suffering and groaning now; both are going to be set free together. As nature shared in the curse, and now shares in the pain, so it will also share in the glory. Hence *the creation waits in eager expectation for the sons of God to be revealed.* And what the creation is looking for is the revelation of God's children, that is, the disclosure of their identity on the one hand and their investiture with glory on the other. This will be the signal for the renewal of the whole creation."
>
> "But what is meant by *the creation*, an expression which occurs four times in verses 19-22, once in each verse? By *the creation*, he will have intended 'the earth, with all it contains, animate and inanimate, man excepted, or 'the sum-total of subhuman nature.'"
>
> Stott, John R. W., ***The Message of Romans***, 1994, InterVarsity Press, England, Illinois, page 238.

Stifler, James Madison

1839 – 1902, Pennsyvania. Graduated from Shurtleff College, Theological course in 1869. Pastor at Hamilton, New York, and New Haven, Connecticut. For 21 years was Professor in Crozer Theological Seminary, Upland, Pennsylvania.

Please see Dr. Stifler's commentary on Romans quoted by Pettingill under our entry for "Pettingill, William Leroy."

Pettingill, William Leroy, ***Simple Studies In Romans***, 1915, Philadelphia School of the Bible, Pennsylvania, pages 110-111.

Thomas, William Henry Griffith

1861 – 1924, England. Rev. W. H. Griffith Thomas, D. D., was an Anglican Clergyman and Scholar from the English-Welsh border country. He was a Professor of Old Testament Literature and Exegesis. In addition to several Pastorates, he taught for several years as Principal of Wycliffe Hall, Oxford, and then at Wycliffe College in Toronto, Canada. He was a co-founder with Lewis Sperry Chafer of Dallas Theological Seminary, and authored several books.

> "The Appeal of Creation (Romans 8:19-22). This glory is actually being awaited with eagerness, even by the irrational creation which is longing for the manifestation of the sons of God (verse 19). Creation is now under the curse of sin, for somehow or other the sin of man has affected the lower orders of creation. Nature is not as it was in its original constitution, but through sin has been "subjected to vanity by reason of God Who subjected it in hope that there would be a deliverance of creation from corruption" into the liberty of the glory of the children of God (verses 20-21). The need of this deliverance is seen by the present condition of creation. We Christians know that the entire creation is groaning and travailing in pain until now. Everything points to the fact that the present constitution of the universe is not what it was at first, or what it will be hereafter; and this state of affairs as occasioned by sin is a clear proof of the glory that yet awaits creation."

> "Very much that we see around us goes to show that nature is not now in a normal condition, or in that state in which it was originally created by God. Physical

suffering among animals, catastrophes and cataclysms in nature have some moral meaning, we may be sure. Scripture is quite clear as to the certainty of 'a good time coming' for the entire universe. Originally creation was 'good,' but it fell when man fell (Genesis 3:17-19), and shall be restored when he is restored (Hebrews 2:5-9). Many passages indicate with unerring clearness the wonderful future for nature as well as for man (Isaiah 11:6-9, Revelation 5:13)."

"Not only does creation groan, waiting for the great future, but believers themselves are longing for that full redemption which will come with the resurrection of the body (Romans 8:23)."

> Thomas, W. H. Griffith, *St. Paul's Epistle to the Romans*, 1956, WM. B. Eerdmans Publishing Company, Michigan, pages 220-221.

Toplady, Augustus Montague

1740 – 1778, Ireland. An Anglican Divine, educated at Westminster and Trinity College, Dublin. He was ordained in 1762 and became Vicar of Harpford with Fenn-Ottery, Devon, in 1766. He is chiefly known as a writer of hymns and poems, including the famous hymn "***Rock of Ages***." He served as Vicar of Broadhembury until his death.

"Romans 8: 19-21, which I would thus render and thus punctuate: The earnestly wishful expectancy of the creation, i.e., of the brute creation; that implicit thirst after happiness, wrought and kneaded into the very being of every creature endued with sensitive life; virtually waits with vehement desire, for that appointed, glorious manifestation of the sons of God, which is to take place in the millenniary state: for the creation, the lower animal creation, was subjected to uneasiness, not willing it, or through any voluntary transgression committed by themselves; but by reason or on account of him who subjected them to pain and death, in hope, and with a view, that this very creation shall likewise be emancipated from the bondage of corruption into the glorious liberty of the children of God. What a field of pleasing and exalted speculation does this open to the benevolent and philosophic mind!"

    Toplady, Augustus Montague, ***The Works of Augustus M. Toplady**, **A.B.***, Chapter: *A Short Essay On Original Sin,* 1825, William Baynes and Son, Edinburgh.

Trench, Richard Chenevix

1807 – 1886, Ireland. Archibishop of Dublin, Church of Ireland. He studied at the schools of Twyford and Harrow, and at Trinity College, Cambridge. Ordained in 1830 and in 1832 became curate to H. J. Rose at Hadleigh, Suffolk, then at Colchester. Ordained a Priest in 1835. Professor of Divinity at King's College, Professor of Exegesis of the New Testament, Dean of Westminster, Archbishop of Dublin.

"Turn your eyes to another province of the kingdom of nature – to the world of animals. Do we not encounter the same discords, the same disharmonious theme? Much, very much, to tell us that the state of Paradise has disappeared, not for man only, but for the whole creation, whose destinies were made dependent upon his, which fell when he fell, and can only rise again when he rises ….. A day, however, is coming – our Lord calls it the 'regeneration,' that is, the new birth of nature, even as there is already a new birth of man – when the curses shall be lightened from the earth, as it has already been lightened from his body; ….. the day when there shall be no more curse, when the wolf shall dwell with the lamb, when the leopard shall lie down with the kid, when they shall not hurt, nor destroy in all

God's Holy mountain, and that Holy mountain shall be as wide as the earth itself."

> Moor, J. Frewen, ***Thoughts Regarding The Future State Of Animals***, From Trench's *"The Groans of Creation*, 1899, Warren & Son Printers and Publishers, London, pages 86-87.

Van Impe, Jack

1930 – Michigan. An evangelist who appears on his weekly television show *Jack Van Impe Presents* with his wife, Rexella. He has been known as the 'walking Bible' because of his extensive memorization of Bible verses. He went to Detroit Bible College. Dr. Van Impe is knowledgeable in virtually every area of Christian living, and is an avid student of Bible prophecy and world events. Several leading seminaries and Bible colleges across America have honored him with doctoral degrees in the field of theology. He is the author of several books and videos.

Dr. Jack Van Impe has a video/DVD called ***Animals In Heaven?*** In it he states that he believes that the Bible clearly states that all animals go to Heaven, and mentioned several theologians that believed this also. Dr. Jack Van Impe believes that the animals are included in the rapture, and indicated that some theologians do as well.

> "I have just finished reading the book and feel that it was well done. I have considered making a video on "Pets in Heaven."
>
> Letter to Niki Behrikis Shanahan reviewing ***There Is Eternal Life For Animals***, October 23, 2002.

Walvoord, John F.

1910 – 2002, Texas. He was a Christian Theologian, Pastor, and President of Dallas Theological Seminary from 1952 to

1986. He was the author of over 30 books, focusing primarily on eschatology and theology including *The Rapture Question*, and was co-editor of *The Bible Knowledge Commentary* with Roy B. Zuck. He earned AB and DD degrees from Wheaton College, an AM degree from Texas Christian University in philosophy, a ThB, ThM, and ThD in Systematic theology from Dallas Theological Seminary, and a LittD from Liberty Baptist Seminary. He pastored the Rosen Heights Presbyterian church in Fort Worth.

In ***An Exposition of the Scriptures by Dallas Seminary Faculty,*** New Testament Edition, Walvoord and Zuck review Romans 8:19-23. They discuss the interrelationship of man with the physical creation, and say that Paul explains that this relationship has a future aspect in connection with God's program of salvation for people. They say that all of nature (inanimate and animate) is personified as waiting eagerly for that time. Since God's program of salvation for people is one of a new Creation, (2 Cor. 5:17; Gal. 6:15), the physical world also will be re-created (Rev. 21:5).

Wesley, John

1703 – 1791, England. An Anglican Minister, Christian Theologian, and Evangelist. Born in England he studied at Westminster School and Christ Church, Oxford. He was ordained Deacon in 1725 and priest in 1728. In 1726 he became a fellow at Oxford and lecturer in Greek. He was a prolific writer, producing grammars, histories, biographies, collections of hymns, his own sermons and journals, and a magazine.

The following is an excerpt from Rev. John Wesley's sermon, ***"The General Deliverance:"***

> "While His creatures 'travail together in pain,' He knoweth all their pain, and is bringing them nearer and nearer to the birth, which shall be accomplished in its season. He seeth 'the earnest expectation' wherewith

the whole animated creation 'waiteth for' that final 'manifestation of the sons of God,' in which 'they themselves also shall be delivered' (not by annihilation; annihilation is not deliverance) from the present bondage of corruption, into a measure of the glorious liberty of the children of God."

"Nothing can be more express: Away with vulgar prejudices, and let the plain Word of God take place. They 'shall be delivered from the bondage of corruption, into glorious liberty,' – even a measure, according as they are capable, – of 'the liberty of the children of God.'"

"To descend to a few particulars: The whole brute creation will then, undoubtedly, be restored, not only to the vigor, strength, and swiftness which they had at their creation, but to a far higher degree of each than they ever enjoyed. They will be restored, not only to that measure of understanding which they had in paradise, but to a degree of it as much higher than that, as the understanding of an elephant is beyond that of a worm. And whatever affections they had in the garden of God, will be restored with vast increase; being exalted and refined in a manner which we ourselves are not now able to comprehend."

Wesley, John, ***The Works Of The Reverend John Wesley, A.M.***, 1840, T. Mason and G. Lane, For The Methodist Episcopal Church, *The General Deliverance*.

The following is a very interesting story from John Wesley's journal recording that he and his horse were healed one day simultaneously.

"1746. Monday, March 17. — I took my leave of Newcastle and set out with Mr. Downes and Mr. Shepherd. But when we came to Smeton, Mr. Downes was so ill that he could go no further. When Mr.

Shepherd and I left Smeton, my horse was so exceedingly lame that I was afraid I must have lain by too. We could not discern what it was that was amiss; and yet he would scarcely set his foot to the ground. By riding thus seven miles, I was thoroughly tired, and my head ached more than it had done for some months. (What I here aver is the naked fact: let every man account for it as he sees good.) I then thought, 'Cannot God heal either man or beast, by any means, or without any?' Immediately my weariness and headache ceased, and my horse's lameness in the same instant. Nor did he halt any more either that day or the next. A very odd accident this also!"

> Wesley, John, ***Journal of John Wesley,*** *Chapter 7, Faith Healing And Wesley*, Christian Classics Ethereal Library, Calvin College, Michigan, www.ccel.org.

Because of his writings, I'm convinced that John Wesley loved animals. Here are some excerpts from his journal that I want to share with you.

> "Monday, July 3. — I rode to Coolylough (where was the quarterly meeting) and preached at eleven and in the evening. While we were singing, I was surprised to see the horses from all parts of the ground gathering about us. Is it true then that horses, as well as lions and tigers have an ear for music?"

> Wesley, John, ***Journal of John Wesley,*** Christian Classics Ethereal Library, Calvin College, Michigan, www.ccel.org.

"Wesley's Experiments with Lions"

"Monday, December 31. — I thought it would be worth while to make an odd experiment. Remembering how surprisingly fond of music the lion at Edinburgh was, I determined to try whether this was the case with all animals of the same kind. I accordingly went to the Tower with one who plays on the German flute. He began playing near four or five lions; only one of these (the rest not seeming to regard it at all) rose up, came to the front of his den, and seemed to be all attention. Meantime, a tiger in the same den started up, leaped over the lion's back, turned and ran under his belly, leaped over him again, and so to and fro incessantly. Can we account for this by any principle of mechanism? Can we account for it at all?"

    Wesley, John, ***Journal of John Wesley,***
    Christian Classics Ethereal Library, Calvin
    College, Michigan, www.ccel.org.

The next two excerpts are from a book entitled ***John Wesley And His Horse*** by T. Ferrier Hulme. This book gives us an awareness of the fact that in Wesley's time, the horse was very much a part of the ministry.

"It is no exaggeration to say that one of God's chief agents and of man's most valuable colleagues in the evangelization of England in the eighteenth century was the horse – a noble animal never put to a nobler use. Without it Wesley could never have done what he did and gone where he willed on his 'Father's business.'" (Page 6)

"After preaching at Wick he 'returned to Bristol time enough to praise God in the great congregation and to preach on '*Thou, Lord, shalt save both man and beast.*'" (Page 44)

    Hulme, T. Ferrier, ***John Wesley And His***
    Horse, 1933, The Epworth Press, London.

Williams, Isaac

1802 – 1865, England. The Rev. Isaac Williams was a prominent member of the Oxford Movement, acquainted with

John Keble and, like other members of the movement, associated with Oxford University. He wrote religious poetry and one of the movement's famous tracts: *"Reserve in Religious Teaching"* and *"Devotional Commentary On The Gospel Narrative."*

> *"For the earnest expectation of the creature waiteth for the manifestation of the sons of God.* The inspired Apostle sees the whole of the creation, like one living being, in intense desire and earnest expectation, stretching forth the head and straining the eyes in awful waiting for something that is to appear. He beholds all things that are around us in one vast image or personification, and in one bold figure or expression he sums up all the appearances of this visible universe; day and night, seasons and years, trees and animals, skies and seas, clouds and rivers, and all the generations of men, the whole of created beings around us, and the human soul, – on all these alike there hangs one awful suspense, looking for the manifestation of God's children."*

> *"For the creature was made subject to vanity, not willingly, but by reason of Him Who hath subjected the same in hope.* For this mysterious subjection to vanity under which the creation labors is evidently one of constraint, from not having its own object in which it can rest; not fulfilling its appropriate end; not finding its true and final good. But God has been pleased to subject it to the same for wise reasons in hope of release, and stamped upon it the expectation of that deliverance which it shall share."*

> *"Because the creature itself also shall be delivered from the bondage of corruption, into the glorious liberty of the children of God.* For vanity and death, which hath passed upon all the visible creation, 'the covering' and 'the vail that is spread over all nations' on account of the fall, shall be done away, this temporal

scene 'as a vesture shall be changed;' and 'a new Heaven and a new earth' shall share in that freedom from sin and death."

Williams, Isaac, *Sermons On The Epistles And Gospels For The Sundays And Holy Days Throughout The Year*, 1882, Rivingtons, London.

Wood, J. G.

1827 – 1889, England. (Rev. John George Wood) Rev. J. G. Wood was a Clergyman, author, and lecturer on Natural History. He was educated at Merton College, Oxford, (B.A., 1848, M.A., 1851) and Christ Church where he worked some time in the anatomical museum under Sir Henry Acland. In 1852 he became Curate of the parish of St. Thomas the Martyr, Oxford, and in 1854 was ordained Priest. He was Chaplain to the Boatmen's Floating Chapel at Oxford, and Chaplain to St. Bartholomew's Hospital. In 1858 he accepted a readership at Christ Church, Newgate Street, and he was Assistant Chaplain to St. Bartholomew's Hospital, London, from 1856 until 1862. Between 1868 and 1876 he held the office of precentor to the Canterbury Diocesan Choral Union. After 1876 he devoted himself to the production of books, and to delivering in all parts of the country lectures on zoology. He was a very prolific writer on natural history. Because he was rather sickly as a child, he was educated at home and spent a great deal of time outdoors. During this time he developed his innate love of all of God's creation. Rev. Wood wrote many books, including *Man and Beast: Here and Hereafter, Bible Animals, Wild Animals Of The Bible, Birds Of The Bible,* and *Domestic Animals Of The Bible.*

The following excerpts are from his book, *Man and Beast: Here and Hereafter,* published in 1874. Rev. Wood went into great detail on this subject, and I have made some selections that I am sharing with you here.

"There is a popular belief – I should rather say a popular tradition – that somewhere in the Scriptures we are taught that, of all living inhabitants of earth, man alone possesses a spirit, and that therefore he alone survives in spirit after the death of the material body. If this were true, there would be no room for argument to those who profess to believe the Scriptures literally, and to base their faith upon that literal belief; and, however such a statement might seem to controvert all ideas of benevolence, justice, and even common sense, such believers would be bound to receive it on trust, and to wait for a future time in which to understand it." (Page 1)

"This belief is almost entirely, if not wholly, due to two passages of Scripture, one being in the Psalms and the other in Ecclesiastes. The former is that which is generally quoted as decisive of the whole question. It runs in the Authorized Version as follows: – 'Nevertheless, man being in honour, abideth not; he is like the beasts that perish' (Psalm 49:13:20)." (Page 2)

"The second passage occurs in Ecclesiastes 3:21: 'Who knoweth the spirit of man that goeth upward, and the spirit of the beast that goeth downward to the earth.'" (Pages 2-3)

"There will then be no doubt that we must believe that beasts have no immortal life. But, if we are to take the literal sense of the Bible, and no other, we are equally bound to believe that man as well as beast has no life after death." (Page 3)

"See, for example, Psalm 6:5: 'In death there is no remembrance of Thee: in the grave, who shall give Thee thanks?' Also, Psalm 88:10-12: 'Wilt Thou show wonders to the dead? Shall the dead arise and praise Thee? Shall Thy loving-kindness be declared in the grave, or Thy faithfulness in destruction? Shall Thy wonders be known in the dark, and Thy righteousness in the land of forgetfulness?' Also, see Psalm 115:17: 'The dead praise not the Lord, neither any that go down into silence.'" (Pages 3-4)

"Also, Psalm 146:3-4: 'Put not your trust in princes, nor in the son of man, in whom there is no help. His breath goeth forth, he returneth to his earth; in that very day his thoughts perish.'" (Page 4)

"In the very book in which occurs the single passage on which is based the denial of the immortality of the animals, are five passages which proclaim the same end to the life of man. We are told distinctly and definitely, that those who have died have no remembrance of God, and cannot praise Him. Death is described as the 'land of forgetfulness,' – the place of darkness, where all man's thoughts perish. Can more than this be said of the 'beasts that perish'?" (Page 5)

"Now we will leave the Psalmist and proceed to other writers. Treating, not of the wicked, but of mankind in general who 'dwell in houses of clay,' the writer proceeds as follows: – 'They are destroyed from morning to evening; *they perish for ever*, without any regarding it' (Job 4:20). Take another passage from the same book, a passage which is even more definite in its statement. 'As the cloud is consumed and vanisheth away, so he that goeth down to the grave shall come up no more' (Job 7:9). Again – 'Man dieth, and wasteth away: yea, man giveth up the ghost, and where is he? As the waters fail from the sea, and the flood decayeth and drieth up:' 'So man lieth down, and riseth not' (Job 14:10-12 and verse 14: 'If a man die, shall he live again?'"(Page 5)

"Turning to the Book of Ecclesiastes, in which occurs the solitary passage which is held to disprove the immortality of the animals, we find the following passages, which are even more emphatic as to the future state of man." (Page 6)

"'I said in my heart concerning the estate of the sons of men, that God might manifest them, and that they might see that they themselves are beasts. For that which befalleth the sons of men befalleth beasts; even one thing befalleth them. As the one dieth, so dieth the other; yea, they have all one breath, so that a man hath no pre-eminence over a beast: for all is vanity. All go unto one place; all are of the dust, and all turn to dust again.'" (Ecclesiastes 3:18-20) (Pages 6-7)

"Also in Ecclesiastes 9:10: 'Whatsoever thy hand findeth to do, do it with thy might; for there is no work, nor device, nor knowledge, nor wisdom in the grave whither thou goest.'" (Page 7)

"Taking the literal sense of these words and no other, it is impossible to doubt their import. They state definitely that, as regards a spiritual life, there is no distinction between man and beast; and that when they die, all go to the same place. The writer also distinctly states that after death man can work nothing, know nothing, nor can receive any reward. The same vein of irrepressible sadness that characterizes the extracts taken from the Psalms is prominent in those passages from Job and Ecclesiastes; and if from these alone we were to deduce our ideas of the condition of man after death, most sad and hopeless would be the very thought of dissolution." (Page 7)

"It is true that we do not accept them in this light, knowing that they are written symbolically or parabolically, and that there underlies them the spiritual sense of which St. Paul speaks when he contrasts the lifegiving spirit with the death-dealing letter (2 Cor. Iv. 6). With that meaning, however, we have in the present case nothing to do. We are only concerned with the literal meaning of our translation, and, according to that literal meaning, if we take two texts to prove that beasts have no future life, we are forced by no less than fourteen passages to believe that man, in common with beasts, has no future life. We have no right to pick and choose which passages we are to take literally, and which symbolically, but must apply the same test to all alike, and treat all in the same manner." (Page 8)

"There is, however, one passage which certainly does seem to point to a future for the beast, as well as for man, and does at all events place them both on a similar level. It occurs in Genesis 9:5, and forms part of the concise law which was delivered to Noah, and which was the forerunner of the fuller law afterwards given through Moses: 'Surely, your blood of your lives will I require; at the hand of every beast will I require it, and at the hand of every man; at the hand of every man's brother will I require the life of man.'"(Page 459)

"And this injunction was afterwards incorporated into the Mosaic law, where an ox who kills a man is subject to death, just as if it had been a man who had murdered one of his fellows (see Exodus 21:28)." (Page 459)

"As a writer in the *London Review* well said, some years ago, 'There would be no meaning in this retribution if the animal had no living soul to be forfeited, as the human soul had been yielded to death.'" (Page 459)

> Wood, J. G., ***Man and Beast: Here and Hereafter,*** 1874, George Routledge and Sons, New York.

His son, Rev. Theodore Wood, F.E.S., wrote a book called ***The Rev. J. G. Wood: His Life and Work***, dated 1890, The Cassell Publishing Company. In reference to his father writing ***Man and Beast: Here and Hereafter***, his son wrote:

"His working copy of 'Man and Beast' is filled with letters from friends and manuscript notes of his own, and he had clearly been collecting material for additions and improvements. And gummed upon the title page is a printed extract from some religious magazine which struck him very deeply, and to which he often referred in the course of conversation. It refers to the original Hebrew of the term translated in our version as "living soul."

"Certain of King James's translators (it says) ... have rendered the Hebrew word 'nephesh,' soul, when referring to man, quite literally. The fact that the *same word* is applied to *animals* is covered up, or concealed, to all who are not Hebrew scholars, other words being substituted for it, such as 'life,' or 'creature.'"

"In Genesis 1:30, 'To every beast of the earth, and to every fowl of the air, and to everything that creepeth upon the earth wherein there is life;' the Hebrew words are 'nephesh chaiyah,' *a living soul*. Also in Genesis 1:20, 'Let the waters bring forth abundantly the moving creature that hath *life*;' literally, *a living soul*."

"Ten times is the Hebrew of 'living soul' found in the first nine chapters of Genesis, and only once, when it refers to man, is it literally translated. In nine other instances, when it refers to the lower orders of creation, is the fact carefully concealed from the readers of the English version. *In seven of the nine instances it is Jehovah who uses this unorthodox language.* Apparently this extract was intended to serve as the foundation of an additional chapter, for I find enclosed in the book a large sheet of carefully worked-out notes, in which a reference to the 'nephesh' of the Hebrew has a very prominent place."

"He would do almost anything for a cat. I have known him to leave his work, and to go down from the top of the house to the bottom, on three separate occasions in the course of a single morning, just because it occurred to one of our cats that she would like to show him her kittens. She would come to the door, and mew for admission, and then sit and mew again until he got up and accompanied her downstairs; and then she would go straight off to the basket where her kittens were lying, and rub herself against it, and then against him, purring loudly, and in every way endeavoring to show her pride. Then he would stroke and admire them, ask the cat whether she were satisfied, and then go back to his work. And in the course of half and hour or so the same programme would be exactly repeated. He would always cheerfully give up his time to supplying the wants of a cat, or indeed of any animal, whether those wants were fancied or real. And he was never more happy than when surrounded by animals with which he was intimate, and which, to him, were not only companions, but true and actual friends."

Wood, Theodore, *The Rev. J. G. Wood: His Life and Work*, 1890, The Cassell Publishing Company, New York, pages 91-95 and 295.

Wordsworth, Christopher

1807 – 1885, England. Christopher Wordsworth, M.A., D.D. was an English Bishop, he was elected a fellow and tutor of Trinity. He then served as Canon of Westminster, Vicar of Stanford in the Vale, Berkshire, and Archdeacon of Westminster. From 1869 till his death in 1885 Wordsworth was Bishop of Lincoln. As a Scholar he is best known for his edition of the *Greek New Testament* (1856-1860), and the *Old Testament* (1864-1870).

"By the sin of the first Adam, not only did death come into the world, but the whole creation, which had been made 'very good' by God, and had been blessed by

Him, was marred and made subject to vanity and to a curse ... But it has been so subjected involuntarily and by no fault of its own; and it has been subjected in a hope, that as it sympathizes with man in his shameful bondage in Adam, so will it also share in his glorious deliverance in Christ."

"To sum up this portion of our argument, Holy Scripture appears to me to assert unhesitatingly that birds and beasts possess spirits or souls, a qualification which of itself makes them suitable subjects for an immortality of existence, and to imply that in a future state they will meet with some compensation for the evils they now suffer."

> Moor, J. Frewen, ***Thoughts Regarding The Future State Of Animals***, 1899, Warren & Son Printers and Publishers, London, page 57.

Zuck, Roy B.

1932 – Arizona. Received B.A. from Biola University and moved to Dallas, Texas to attend Dallas Theological Seminary. He completed his Th.M. in 1957, majoring in Old Testament. Served as executive Vice President of Scripture Press Ministries from 1965-73. Then he accepted a teaching position at Moody Bible Institute in Chicago, and then began teaching at Dallas Seminary. Roy B. Zuck is Senior Professor Emeritus of Biblical Exposition at Dallas Theological Seminary. He has authored or edited more than 70 books on Christian Education and Bible exposition.

Please see entry under "Walvoord, John" from ***An Exposition of the Scriptures by Dallas Seminary Faculty,*** New Testament Edition.

Other Commentaries

Carrington, Edith

1853 – 1929, England. Edith Carrington was the author of several animal books, and she was the editor of *Thoughts Regarding The Future State Of Animals.*

> "For those whose hearts are prepared to receive it, there runs throughout Holy Scripture a complete Gospel for 'the creature,' a glad tidings of everlasting life."

> "In a set of tracts by that well known and interesting writer about animals, Miss Edith Carrington, called *The Creatures Delivered Into Our Hands*, published by Griffith, Farran, & Co., we find the following passage bearing on the subject before us: Where is the song of universal praise which St. John heard every creature singing, 'on earth and under the earth, and such as are in the sea, and all that are in them,' the harmony which ought to be swelling up to His Throne, even now the foretaste of what will be more perfectly? It was given to the Disciple to learn by that marvelous vision in Patmos what the eternal destiny was of animals, which now man treads under his feet, namely, to praise God eternally, saying: 'Blessing and honor and glory and power be unto Him that sitteth upon the Throne, and unto the Lamb for ever and ever.'"

> Moor, J. Frewen, *Thoughts Regarding The Future State Of Animals*, 1899, Warren & Son Printers and Publishers, London, Editorial note and page 83.

Colam, John

1827 – 1910, England. Secretary of the Royal Society for the Prevention of Cruelty to Animals (RSPCA), 1860–1905; editor, *Animal World*, 1869–1905; *Band of Mercy*, 1880–1905. One of the founders of the Battersea Dogs' Home and the National Society for the Prevention of Cruelty to Children. Personally stopped a bullfight from taking place in London in 1870, and was later awarded a gold medal by the Paris SPCA and a gold watch by the RSPCA for his courage. Received the first Queen's medal given for conspicuous service to the RSPCA, and was a strong anti-vivisection supporter.

> "Many Divines had asserted the doctrine of the immorality of animals, even going so far as to establish it from the immortality of man; and humanitarians, joining in such contention, submit an argument in favor of the rights of animals, based on the circumstance that they are not merely beasts which perish, but, according to the Bible, they derive their lives from the same source which giveth life to human beings; that they are dependent on the same laws of health; and that what befalls them in death, befalls man also."
>
> Moor, J. Frewen, ***Thoughts Regarding The Future State Of Animals***, extract of speech by John Colam, Esq., from *Animal World*, April 1894, 1899, Warren & Son Printers and Publishers, London, page 97.

Dixon, Royal

1885 – 1962, Texas. An American author educated at the Sam Houston Normal Institute, and as a special student at the University of Chicago. After spending five years with the department of botany at the Field Museum of Chicago, he entered the literary field as a member of the *Houston Chronicle* staff. He made special contributions to the newspapers of New York, where he lectured for the Board of Education. Dixon wrote several books, such as, ***The Human Side of Animals***, and ***The Human Side of Birds.***

"The old belief is still prevalent that the Bible teaches that of all living creatures man alone is immortal. This erroneous belief springs out of man's egotism, however, and is not substantiated by the Scriptures. Among many of the Old Testament writers we find that immortality was assured for neither man nor animals; whereas, with the larger revelation of the New Testament, immortality is no longer questioned for any living creature."

Dixon, Royal, ***The Human Side of Animals***, 1918, Frederick A. Stokes Company Publishers, New York.

'Tis always morning somewhere, and above'
The awakening continents, from shore to shore,
Somewhere the birds are singing evermore.
Henry Wadsworth Longfellow

Dixon, Royal, ***The Human Side of Birds***, 1917, Halcyon House, New York.

Springer, Rebecca Ruter

1832 – 1904, Indiana. Rebecca was an author, a very devout Christian, and the daughter of Rev. Calvin W. Ruter, a prominent Methodist Clergyman in Indiana. Rebecca married William McKendree Springer, a judge and a member of congress for many years.

Over one hundred years old, ***Intra Muros*** is a classic book in the Christian tradition. While on her deathbed, Rebecca experienced a vision. After several days she recovered and returned from her vision in Heaven. As she did recover from her illness, she felt that this vision was given as an example of what Heavenly life is like. Or put in other words, if she stayed in Heaven and did not return to tell the story, this is the scenario of your life in your transition from earth life to Heavenly life. The author states "I may be able to partly tear the veil from the death we so dread, and show it to be only an open door into a new and beautiful phase of the life we now live." While she was in Heaven her brother-in-law said, "If only we could realize while we are yet mortals, that day by day we are building for eternity, how different our lives in many ways would be!"

I would like to share some excerpts from her book called *Intra Muros*, which is Greek for "within the walls." Rebecca Ruter Springer wrote it in 1898. The first one is regarding her deceased pet dog.

> "Not far from our home we saw a group of children playing upon the grass, and in their midst was a beautiful great dog, over which they were rolling and tumbling with the greatest freedom. As we approached he broke away from them and came bounding to meet us, and crouched and fawned at my feet with every gesture of glad welcome."
>
> "Do you not know him, auntie? Mae asked brightly. It is dear old Sport! I cried, stooping and placing my arms about his neck, and resting my head on his silken hair. Dear old fellow! How happy I am to have you here!"
>
> "He responded to my caresses with every expression of delight, and Mae laughed aloud at our mutual joy."
>
> "I have often wondered if I should not some day find him here. He surely deserves a happy life for his faithfulness and devotion in the other life. His

intelligence and his fidelity were far above those of many human beings whom we count immortal."

"Did he not sacrifice his life for little Will? Yes; he attempted to cross the track in front of an approaching train, because he saw it would pass between him and his little master, and feared he was in danger. It cost his life. He always placed himself between any of us and threatened danger, but Will he seemed to consider his special charge. He was a gallant fellow – he deserves immortality. Dear, dear old Sport, you shall never leave me again! I said, caressing him fondly."

"At this he sprang to his feet, barking joyously, and galloped and frolicked before us the rest of the way home, then lay down upon the doorstep, with an upward glance and a wag of his bushy tail, as though to say, 'See how I take you at your word!'"

The second excerpt is regarding a child reunited with a deceased pet cat.

"I remember once seeing a beautiful little girl enter Heaven, the very first to come of a large and affection family. I afterward learned that the sorrowful cry of her mother was, 'Oh, if only we had someone there to meet her, to care for her!' She came, lovingly nestled in the Master's own arms, and a little later, as he sat, still caressing and talking to her, a remarkably fine Angora kitten, of which the child had been very fond, and which had sickened and died some weeks before, to her great sorrow, came running across the grass and sprang directly into her arms, where it lay contentedly. Such a glad cry as she recognized her little favorite, such a hugging and kissing as that kitten received, made joy even in Heaven! Who but our loving Father would have thought of such comfort for a little child?"

Springer, Rebecca Ruter, ***Intra Muros,*** 1898, David C. Cook Publishing Company.

Bibliography

Arrington, French L., *Creation's Hopeful Expectation: An Exegesis of Romans 8:19-22*, 1972, Tennessee.

Booth, William, *Visions*, 1906, The Salvation Army Printing Works, St. Albans.

Brown, David; Jamieson, Robert; Fausset, A. R., *Commentary, Critical, Experimental, and Practical, on the Old and New Testaments*, The Epistle of Paul the Apostle to the Romans, 1871. Christian Classics Ethereal Library, Calvin College, Michigan, www.ccel.org.

Bruce, F. F., *The Epistle Of Paul To The Romans*, 1980, Wm. B. Eerdmans Publishing Company, Michigan.

Calvin, John, *Commentary on Romans*, Christian Classics Ethereal Library, Calvin College, Michigan, www.ccel.org.

Carter, William, *Expects To Meet Animals In Heaven*, January 31, 1927, *New York Times*.

Chalmers, Thomas, *Lectures Of The Epistle Of Paul The Apostle To The Romans*, 1874, Robert Carter & Brothers, New York.

Clarke, Adam, *The Holy Bible, Containing The Old And New Testaments With A Commentary And Critical Notes by Adam Clarke, LL.D., F.A.S.*, 1854, William Tegg And Co, London.

Cranfield, C. E. B., *Romans A Shorter Commentary*, 1985, William B. Eerdmans Publishing Company, Michigan.

Criswell, W. A. *"What I Believe About Heaven: The Inexpressible Preciousness,"* June 24, 1990, and *Redemptive Suffering*, 10/17/54. www.wacriswell.org, Texas.

Darby, John Nelson, *Synopsis to the Books of the Bible, Romans*, Christian Classics Ethereal Library, Calvin College, Michigan, www.ccel.org.

De Haan, M. R., **Studies in Revelation**, 1946, Published by Kregel Publications, Grand Rapids, Michigan. Used by permission of the publisher. All rights reserved.

Dixon, Royal, **The Human Side of Animals**, 1918, Frederick A. Stokes Company Publishers, New York.

Dixon, Royal, **The Human Side of Birds**, 1917, Halcyon House, New York.

Fowle, Edmund, **Plain Preaching For A Year**, 1873, *The Future Of Creation by Rev. S. Baring-Gould, M.A.*, W. Skeffington, Piccadilly, London.

Fuller, Andrew, **Dialogues, Letters, and Essays On Various Subjects**, 1810, Oliver D. Cooke, New York.

Fulton, John S., *The New York Times*, **On Kindness To Animals**, November 19, 1899.

Hahne, Harry Alan, **The Corruption And Redemption Of Creation: Nature in Romans 8.19-22 and Jewish Apocalyptic Literature**, 2006, T&T Clark, London, New York.

Hammond, Peter, **The Bible And Animals**, 1984, Frontline Fellowship, South Africa, http://www.thebibleandanimals.org/.

Headlam, Arthur Cayley; Sanday, William, **The International Critical Commentary on the Holy Scriptures of the Old and New Testaments, The Epistle To The Romans**, 1896, Charles Scribner's Sons, New York.

Henry, Matthew, **Commentary of the Whole Bible Volume VI (Acts to Revelation), Romans**; **Commentary of the Whole Bible Volume III (Job to Song of Solomon), Proverbs**, Christian Classics Ethereal Library, Calvin College, Michigan, www.ccel.org.

Hulme, T. Ferrier, **John Wesley And His Horse**, 1933, The Epworth Press, London.

Johnson, Barton W., **The People's New Testament**, *Commentary of Romans*, 1891.

Josephus, Flavius, ***Discourse To The Greeks Concerning Hades***, Christian Classics Ethereal Library, Calvin College, Michigan, www.ccel.org.

Lindsay, Gordon, ***Difficult Questions About The Bible Answered***, 1986, Christ For The Nations, Texas.

Lloyd-Jones, D. Martyn, ***Romans: Exposition of Chapter 8:17-39, The Final Perseverance of the Saints***, 1976, Zondervan Publishing House, Grand Rapids, Michigan.

Luther, Martin, ***Luther's Works, I Corinthians 7, I Corinthians 15, Lectures on I Timothy***, 1973, Concordia Publishing House, Saint Louis.

MacDonald, George, ***The Hope Of The Gospel***, 1892, www.gutenberg.org, Utah.

Marvin, Frederic Rowland, ***Christ Among The Cattle***, 1912, Sherman, French & Company, Boston.

McGee, J. Vernon, ***Thru The Bible Commentary Series, The Epistles, Romans Chapters 1-8***, 1991, Thomas Nelson Publishers, Nashville, Atlanta, London, Vancouver.

McGee, J. Vernon, ***Thru The Bible Commentary Series, Revelation Chapters 1-5***, 1991, Thomas Nelson Publishers, Nashville, Atlanta, London, Vancouver.

Moor, J. Frewen, ***Thoughts Regarding The Future State Of Animals***, 1899, Warren & Son Printers and Publishers, London.

Moorehead, William G., ***Outline Studies In Acts, Romans, First And Second Corinthians, Galatians And Ephesians***, 1902, Fleming H. Revell Company, Chicago, New York, Toronto.

Newell, William R., ***Romans Verse-By-Verse***, Christian Classics Ethereal Library, Calvin College, Michigan, www.ccel.org.

Pettingill, William Leroy, **Simple Studies In Romans**, 1915, Philadelphia School of the Bible, Pennsylvania.

Phillips, Forbes Alexander, **Athol Forbes On Animals**, 1898, *The London Daily Mail.*

Pusey, Edward Bouverie, **Our Animal Friends** (A Monthly Magazine published by The American Society for the Prevention of Cruelty to Animals), 1893, New York.

Pym, William Wollaston, **The Restitution Of All Things**, 1843, James Nisbet And Co., London.

Shanahan, Niki Behrikis, **There Is Eternal Life For Animals**, 2002, Pete Publishing, Massachusetts.

Springer, Rebecca Ruter, **Intra Muros,** 1898, David C. Cook Publishing Company.

Stott, John R. W., **The Message of Romans**, 1994, InterVarsity Press, England, Illinois.

Thomas, W. H. Griffith, **St. Paul's Epistle to the Romans**, 1956, WM. B. Eerdmans Publishing Company, Michigan.

Toplady, Augustus Montague, **The Works of Augustus M. Toplady**, Chapter: *A Short Essay On Original Sin,* 1825, William Baynes and Son, Edinburgh.

Van Impe, Jack, **Animals In Heaven?**, Jack Van Impe Ministries, Michigan. (DVD/video).

Walvoord, John F.; Zuck, Roy B., **An Exposition of the Scriptures by Dallas Seminary Faculty,** New Testament Edition, 1983, Victor Books, A Division of SP Publications, Inc., Illinois.

Wesley, John, **The Works Of The Reverend John Wesley, A.M.,** T. Mason and G. Lane, For The Methodist Episcopal Church, *The General Deliverance*, 1840.

Williams, Isaac, ***Sermons On The Epistles And Gospels For The Sundays And Holy Days Throughout The Year***, 1882, Rivingtons, London.

Wood, J. G., ***Man and Beast: Here and Hereafter***, 1874, George Routledge and Sons, New York.

Wood, Theodore, ***The Rev. J. G. Wood: His Life and Work***, 1890, The Cassell Publishing Company, New York.

Resources

The Living Bible, Tyndale House Publishers, 1971, Illinois.

King James Version, B. B. Kirkbride Bible Co., Inc., 1964, Indiana.

The Christian Classics Ethereal Library, Calvin College, Michigan. A non-profit organization providing free electronic books, www.ccel.org.

The Project Gutenberg Literary Archive Foundation, Utah. A non-profit educational corporation offering free electronic books, www.gutenberg.org.

Wikipedia is a free online encyclopedia and reference website. http://en.wikipedia.org/wiki/Main_Page

Who Says Animals Go To Heaven?
*A Collection Of Prominent Christian Leaders' Beliefs
In Life After Death For Animals.*

The Rainbow Bridge: Pet Loss Is Heaven's Gain
Pet loss support from a Christian perspective.

There Is Eternal Life For Animals
Proves through Bible Scripture that all animals go to Heaven.

Animal Prayer Guide
Prayers and blessings for your pet that you can use everyday.

You may order these titles by visiting us at www.eternalanimals.com or contact the publisher at:

Niki Behrikis Shanahan
Pete Publishing
P. O. Box 282
Tyngsborough, MA 01879

Email: eternalanimals@comcast.net
We welcome you to visit us at:
www.eternalanimals.com

Our website is dedicated to animals and pets with a focus on animal afterlife from a Christian perspective, prayer for pets, and animal appreciation. You'll find articles, stories, news, health and wellness information, photos, and other resources. We welcome prayer requests for animals.

God Bless You And Your Family!